Directions in Technical Writing and Communication

Baywood's Technical Communications Series

Edited by Jay R. Gould

Baywood Publishing Company, Inc.
Farmingdale, N.Y. 11735

Library of Congress Catalog Card Number: 77-075832
ISBN Number: 0-89503-006-3

© 1978, Baywood Publishing Company, Inc.

Library of Congress Cataloging in Publication Data
Main entry under title:

Directions in technical writing and communication.

  (Baywood's technical communications series ; no. 1)
    1. Technical writing. 2. Communication of technical information. I. Gould, Jay Reid.
T11.D54   808'.066'6021   77-75832
ISBN 0-89503-006-3

Table of Contents

Preface

Teachers of technical writing are frequently handicapped by a lack of material to back up discussions in the classroom and in textbooks. *Directions in Technical Writing and Communication* will help, we hope, to overcome this weakness.

Technical and science writers, and other professionals who spend a considerable amount of time in communicating, find that they could benefit by new and authoritative resource material. *Directions in Technical Writing and Communication* should be a great help to them.

From these readings, students will discover that the principles learned in class can be carried over into their careers. They can see how both teachers and practicing writers solve various writing problems.

The book, then, can be used in several ways: as an adjunct to a standard textbook to provide authoritative examples of practices and techniques and as a resource book in companies and government agencies to show writers and other communicators what is being done in technical communication. The readings will impress on students the value of clear, dynamic, and well organized professional writing; and the selections will make a valuable reference book in documentation and library services.

The articles have been selected from more than two hundred published in the *Journal of Technical Writing and Communication* over a seven-year period. They have been chosen to illustrate the theme of this first book in a contemplated series: avenues to be taken in reaching a stage of competence. Each article deserves a wide circulation.

What more appropriate as a title than *Directions*? In these readings a number of principles are discussed in specific ways. First comes a topic that cannot be ignored: what is technical writing? Once this has been established, the reader is introduced to four aspects of the subject: reports, proposals, professional papers, and presentations. Then the industrial writers take over with their articles ranging through the practical: how to edit, and how to prepare special kinds of communication. The book closes with ideas from various sources on evaluation, readability, and motivation.

We would like to comment on each of the contributors, but space is not available. Each of them has written with one objective in mind: to keep the message precise and exact and to pass on expertise to others. Needless to say, all are recognized as authorities in their fields. We are grateful to them for letting us have an insight into their experiences.

PART ONE

What Is Technical Communication?

CHAPTER 1

A New Approach
to Effective Writing*

ROBERT R. RATHBONE
Professor of Literature
Department of Humanities
Massachusetts Institute of Technology

While enroute to a seminar in California last spring, I was asked by a fellow passenger what I did for a living. When I explained that I taught technical writing at MIT, he stared at me for a moment and then remarked: "Good Lord, don't tell me they *teach* engineers to write that way."

Although his remark was intended as friendly humor, it became clear as our conversation continued that he shared the unfortunate impression still held by a large segment of the general public—engineers and scientists can't write. Because the trip lasted only five hours, I'm afraid I was unable to make him change his mind.

Naturally, I reject any notion that relegates technical students to the rank of illiterate. But I do not wish to imply that technical writing is intrinsically good writing. Indeed, there is abundant evidence that it still needs to be improved at all levels, not just

*The suggestions presented in this article are drawn from a book by the author, *Communicating Technical Information: A Guide to Current Uses and Abuses in Scientific and Engineering Writing*, Addison-Wesley, Reading, Mass., 1966.

at the undergraduate level. Technical people on the whole readily admit the deficiency; however, seldom do they force themselves to do something positive about it. Some students, in fact, seem to be easily persuaded to settle for a peaceful coexistence with the English language.

The following suggestions are intended as a plan of attack for engineers and scientists, young or old, who are willing to take the initiative.

Writing as a Problem in Communications

My first suggestion is to approach a writing problem as you would a problem in engineering or design. Whenever you write a technical report, you involve yourself and your reader in many communication functions. These functions constitute the basic elements of a communications system; therefore, the better you understand the systems the better you will be able to satisfy the requirements of any given assignment.

It is not necessary to construct a mathematical model in order to understand the theory involved. The simple block diagram presented by Messrs. Claude Shannon and Warren Weaver in *The Mathematical Theory of Communication*[1] will serve the purpose nicely.

Their system, as shown in Figure 1, consists of five distinct elements:

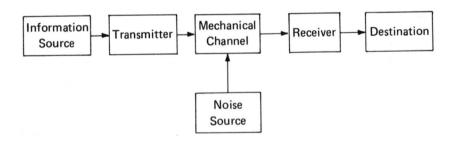

Figure 1. Shannon-Weaver mechanical communications system.

The Information Source provides the inputs from which a message is formed.

The Transmitter transforms the message into signals and transfers the signals to a distribution medium.

The Mechanical Channel is the means for carrying the signals to a receiver.

The Receiver reconstructs the signals into the original message.

The Destination translates the message into meaningful information.

Shannon and Weaver used the diagram to describe the operation of a telephone system. Their concept of noise in the mechanical channel is readily understood within this context, since in practice such a system would not be noise-free.

Using this first diagram as a point of departure, we can now construct a simple model of a system that employs the written report as the communication channel (Figure 2). At the originating end there are three elements instead of two: an

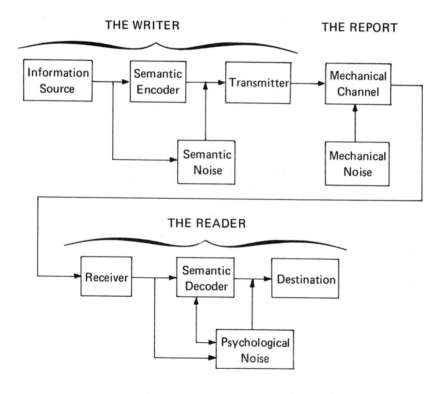

Figure 2. Technical report as a communications system.

Information Source, a *Semantic Encoder,* and a *Transmitter.* Together they constitute the functions that must be performed by the writer. The Information Source is the mind of the writer, assisted by external memory devices such as notes, data sheets, and other reports. It selects the message to be transmitted and determines the thesis and intent. The Semantic Encoder selects the type of channel to be used (formal report, informal memorandum, journal article, etc.) and "codes" the message into appropriate mental symbols (words, numbers, mathematical symbols, etc.). The Transmitter performs the physical act of changing the symbols into the graphic signals that appear on the pages of the writing.

The element in the middle, the *Mechanical Channel,* is the finished written report. Its design characteristics are a composite of:

1. the characteristics of the signals it carries,
2. the structures (grammatical, logical, mechanical) into which these signals are placed,
3. the organizational structure of the subject matter, and
4. the physical format itself.

At the receiving end, the three elements (*Receiver, Semantic Decoder,* and *Destination*) represent the multiple functions of the reader. First, he reads the signals, sending them to the brain as coded symbols. Next, he translates the symbols into a message. And finally, he interprets the message, reconstructing the writer's thesis and intent and deciding what to do with the information received.

Noise, unfortunately, can (and does) originate within this system. *Semantic Noise* includes faulty word choice (resulting in ambiguity, wordiness, and vagueness), improper sentence and paragraph structure, failure to put thoughts into a context consistent with the experience of the reader, and poor organization of material. *Mechanical Noise* includes spelling errors, errors or inconsistencies in typography, sloppy layout of illustrations, overcrowding of text on a page, and any physical property that might slow the reader down or cause him to misread. *Psychological Noise* is any emotional reaction by the reader that reduces his ability to reconstruct the message properly. Doubt, boredom, disagreement, anger, and indifference are the common negative reactions of technical readers. The source may be the message itself, the semantic or mechanical noise in the system, or some external stimulus.

The writer is the primary instigator of all noise. He alone is responsible for any semantic noise that creeps into his writing, because he is the one who generates it. He also must be held responsible for any mechanical noise in the system, even though it may be generated by others (e.g., the typist, the draftsman, the printer). Moreover, he is directly responsible for any psychological noise at the receiving end if he has not carefully identified his reader's needs and attempted to meet them. A reasonable conclusion is that the writer must achieve a favorable signal-to-noise ratio in his message if he is to communicate successfully. In general, readers do not expect inexperienced writers to produce noise-free communications. However, they do expect a signal level that will permit them to reconstruct the original message easily.

The key to successful operation of the system, then, is control of noise. The suggestions that follow relate directly to that problem.

Establish the Proper Interface

There is no feedback loop in a writer-reader communication system, so if you are to match your output impedance with the input impedance of your receiver you must put yourself in his place. What is his technical background? His job? His interests? His purpose in reading your report? What services will he expect from you, the writer?

The answer to the last question, of course, is that he will expect many of the things that you expect from the authors of the communications you read:

A title that represents the true coverage of the subject.

An abstract that summarizes the high points, giving quantitative information whenever possible.

An introduction that provides sufficient briefing on the problem and purpose so that the discourse can be followed intelligently.

An orderly presentation of the evidence, emphasized by judicious use of headings and subheadings, that proceeds from the familiar to the unfamiliar, from the whole to the parts.

A clear separation of fact and opinion.

An evaluation that follows logically from the facts and that leads logically to any recommendations.

A clear, readable style that incorporates visual aids wherever verbal signals are inadequate or cumbersome.

A division of the subject matter that will show what material is primary and what is secondary.

Control Psychological Noise

A primary need of any reader of technical material is to be able to follow the subject matter without being distracted or annoyed by the method the author uses to develop it. Yet some authors handle their papers as though they were writing a mystery story. They begin with a baffling title, they withhold a few pertinent facts in the introduction, they include extraneous information, they report false leads, they build up undue suspense, they assign an inordinate amount of space to subplots, and they leave some of their own questions unanswered. In short, they make the reader play detective and solve the case for himself.

Nor is the trouble limited to their coverage and organization of a subject. They frequently cause even more damage with the way they express themselves. Presumably no writer wants to insult his reader, intentionally or unintentionally. Still, one of the quickest ways to achieve the result is to tell the reader that something is *obvious* or *clear*—when to him it isn't obvious or clear at all. Repeated often enough, the ruse will produce unbearable psychological noise and eventually succeed in frustrating him completely. The following are sobering examples:

- *It should be obvious* from the summarizing equations in the appendix that resonance is achieved through direct gamma-ray interactions.

- Although the tests were inconclusive, *it is clear that* the over-all project was a success.

- *As you can readily see*, the factorial design makes very efficient use of the information in each run and reveals the presence of interaction between factors, each based on a variety of experimental conditions.

Similarly, nothing can destroy a reader's confidence more effectively than the feeling that the writer is trying to deceive him. Any attempt to belittle difficulties is bound to create a bad impression. The following examples of "weasel words" are borrowed from the *Style Guide* of the Aerojet-General Corporation:

> The test was very successful except that a rapid structural failure occurred.
>
> Six tests were conducted and the firing curves were smooth for all, except the first, third, fourth, and sixth.
>
> A pressure surge occurred. A search for the missing parts was initiated.

Avoid euphemisms at all times. In reporting failures and setbacks, tell the reader what went wrong, why it went wrong, and what will be done about it. Tell him in unadorned, straightforward language. He might not rejoice at the outcome, but at least he won't accuse you of trying to save your own skin at his expense.

Also try to avoid using meaningless qualifiers. They give the impression that you are afraid of going out on a limb (which you probably are, but why tell the reader!). Here are some favorites:

> well under . . . (as in "well under cost")
> reasonably . . . (as in "reasonably sure")
> rather . . . (as in "rather deadly poison")
> not too . . . (as in "not too accurate")
> more or less . . . (as in "more or less insane")
> considerable . . . (as in "a considerable number")

Furthermore, never tell a reader that the data *seem* to indicate something or that the equipment *tended* to fail, or that, *as far as you know*, the results of your experiment are accurate.

Be Yourself

Young engineers and scientists are particularly susceptible to the idea that they must conform to a conventional image if they are to be accepted as professional persons. And, unfortunately, this usually means that they sacrifice originality and write the way they think their image would write.

For example, some of them believe that a professional person must *sound professional*. I have no idea what this means, but their writing suggests that they believe technical writing cannot be natural, straightforward, or easy to read. They prefer the long word to the short, they revel in jargon and clichés, they replace the active voice with the passive, they turn short sentences into long paragraphs, and they load the message unnecessarily with equations. In other words, they "professionalize" their writing.

Still others are firmly convinced that writing carries more weight if it has a scholarly ring. A scholarly work deserves scholarly treatment, but this does not mean that style should be used simply for style's sake. Nevertheless, the members of this cult choose words that they hope will impress the reader with their erudition. They include innumerable footnotes and references (some that are unnecessary, others that should be part of the text). They construct a massive bibliography. They tailor the message to fit the syntax, not the other way around. They outlaw the pronoun "I." Here is a mild sample; ironically, it comes from the pen of an experienced writer:

> "This issue is our last as editor of the — — —, for in August we start at the — — — University Press as assistant director. Our successor is — — —, an able publisher with excellent experience. . . . Our vacation will be carefree in knowing that he will take over the editorship. . . ."

And finally there are a few who believe that terseness is next to godliness. They have a special talent for brevity, but in their desire to be economical they frequently sacrifice both clarity and readability. They mean well; they're earnest, hard-working individuals—liked by everyone except their readers—but they have the strange notion that "objectivity" and "economy of speech" are one. To them, the model writer must be an efficiency expert.

So I would conclude with this admonition: when you write, be yourself, not a stereotype. Write to enlighten, not to mystify; to inform not to impress; to convey, not to economize. The writing job will turn out to be much less of a chore.

REFERENCE

1. *The Mathematical Theory of Communication*, University of Illinois Press, 1949.

PART TWO

Basic
Forms
of
Technical
Communication

CHAPTER 2

Voracities
and Verities
Are sometimes
Interacting*
(with apologies to Marianne Moore)

DR. LIONEL D. WYLD
Naval Underwater
Systems Center Headquarters
Newport, Rhode Island

"Nullum est iam dictum quod non dictum sit prius."
—Terence

"Sachaiichi."
—current Japanese for "biggest, longest, highest, greatest," etc.

"May your camel fail his next hump inspection."
—Carnack the Magnificent

*From an address presented at the 18th Annual Technical Writers' Institute.

"You mean you want the revised revision of the original revised revision revised?" runs a gag which went the rounds some years ago. Well, report writing today reflects something of this feeling of the perplexed report writer/editor, while at the same time definite indicators are apparent that those who must write reports—that, indeed, the entire field of technical writing—are more sophisticated, more educated, and more seriously concerned with effective communication than writers of a decade ago.

Professional and scientific writing—including "report writing," "technical writing," and "research editing"—has, within the last decade, obviously come into its own; the proliferation of writers' conferences and of textual materials in the field testifies to this status. Where textbooks once bore routine titles like *Composition for Technical Students, Guide to Report Writing, Report Preparation, Technical Writers' Handbook,* and *Writing Scientific Papers and Reports,* trade books now glisten with the language of the new mode: "principles," (*Principles of Scientific and Technical Writing*); "craft," (*The Craft of Technical Writing*), and "creative," (*Creative Report Writing*). The last named work, to quote the publishers, "emphasizes the role of the *creative* report in business and the professions," and speaks of reports that "must be shaped *imaginatively.*" [Italics mine.] Report writing, so long practiced and taught as an applied field, seems now, admittedly, to have much in common with other forms of writing. Today, the fact is generally accepted—though certain educators see a schism developing—that professional, scientific, and industrial writing are not unique endeavors demanding unique techniques. Oh, of course, there is a difference—and I was tempted to say "demanding *somewhat* unique techniques," but then one must recall John Kiernan's classic remark about never finding a woman who was "somewhat pregnant"! Persons in industry, government, and science do face a myriad of communications problems which pose special requirements for their solution, but the communication matrix (reader/writer/vehicle/technique) for one situation has much in common with that for any other situation.

There is, here, no need to discuss the by-now clichés of the field of report writing—Professor Robert Aurner's six or seven "C-Qualities" (Clearness, Conciseness, Correctness, Concreteness, etc.), Professor Wentworth K. Brown's "Six P's of Professional Prose" (Picture the Reader, Plan, Put It Precisely, Prune, etc.), or the late Porter G. Perrin's levels of usage. As long ago as 1959, my article, "Report Writing Need Not Be Dull," called for concepts of effectiveness, personality, and perspective which now appear in various textbooks. The report writing process continues to warrant discussion and study, however, for professionally aware technical writers or editors are probably (to quip on the old adage) made, not born.

A report writer must always keep in mind certain of the old axioms. Basic considerations—even in this age when so humanities-oriented a journal as *The Shakespeare Newsletter* brings forth a Special Computer Issue—must be met.

Relationship of the Material to Your Objectives

This obviously involves thought on the part of the one preparing a report. Basically, technical prose does differ from its more literary counterpart. As Professor Sterling Olmsted outlined it in a lecture in the pioneer Technical Writers' Institute a number of years ago, where the latter is *impressionistic, sensory, associative,* and *subjective,* with the aim of creating an experience, the former is *analytical, conceptual, systematic,* and *objective*; its primary aim is to create an understanding of subject matter. A writer in industry must proceed carefully and conscientiously to organize, to structure—to provide, in other words, an overall arrangement of his material. Some administrators, no matter what you do, will find fault. The head of one of the programs at Syracuse once told a colleague that the second draft of a committee report was better than the first. "It was meaningless before," he said; "at least it's organized meaninglessness now."

Following an assessment of audience and purpose—the basic considerations for *any* writer—other factors must be considered. Among these are 1) density or redundancy, and 2) concreteness or abstractness of the writing. Redundancy has been found helpful but not essential, provided the basic information appears in any given piece of writing; however, in most cases the reader will balk, sometimes seriously, if the material appears in too dense a form. The average reader simply doesn't want to work his "grey cells" too hard. Concreteness involves the use of particular statements with bits of explanatory data to illustrate and particularize; its opposite, the abstract style of writing, often seems to say little because of the generalities which comprise it. At one installation, a draft I had written came back from an engineer with the comment, "I feel we should sprinkle

applications throughout"; he provided a number of "for instances" which made what I had originally written a much more
useful document. As the poet Marianne Moore put it,

*Be abstract
And you'll wish you'd been specific; it's a fact.*

Some attention must be paid, of course, to the internal
arrangement of the material, as well as to overall structure. Basic
paragraphing often poses a problem today simply because higher
education considers passé the traditional rhetoric-and-
composition experiences which were, regardless of their effect
on students' nerves (and instructors' time), quite salutary on the
writing! In education circles, we are becoming experientially
oriented to a fault; while some of it is good, some of it is
"copping out" by the instructors—no help to a student's mastery
of language usage.

How many of you really consider paragraphs any more?
Introductory and concluding paragraphs to given pieces of
writing should be done thoughtfully and well; intermediate
paragraphs should be developed soundly, preferably each with a
single idea presented in a general statement that occurs in a
structurally significant place within the paragraph. The "loose"
paragraph, one haphazardly thrown together and begun and
ended almost at random, can never contribute to an effective
report. Transitions, both between paragraphs and within them
(from sentence to sentence) come with effort, but the effort
pays much in reader ease and in making one's writing fully
effective as an informative document.

Technical Accuracy

It goes without saying that in such a field as report writing,
technical accuracy must achieve perfection. Check both the
subject matter accuracy and that of the writing itself. (A report
writer is thus always the editor of his own material, even though
the organizational plan includes persons whose job it is to edit
and polish.) The true professional relies upon his own knowledge
and checks everything that goes out over his name or from his
desk.

The stories are legion regarding *faux pas* that create problems,
such as the writer who left off a cipher, so that 100,000 became
10,000. Even a minor substitution can prove highly disadvanta-

geous. Consider this sentence from a telephone company document:

> The ordinary telephone contains 475 parts. There are 87 in the dial unit, 75 in the handset, 73 in the ringer, and 108 in the electrical network.

Sound fine? If you'll do a little quick arithmetic, you'll find 132 parts not accounted for!

Technical accuracy involves checking—and double-checking—any figures, math, diagrams, dimensions, etc. If you, as a report writer, don't have the expertise, get an engineer to do it with you. As I used to tell my CE's at Rensselaer, there's no such thing as a 99 per cent perfect bridge. It either *is* a bridge or it isn't. The same perfection should be demanded in report writing.

Readability

There are several theories about readability, and the Flesches and the Gunnings have had their day; they are not unimportant, but some of them represent "misapplied ingenuity"; or, as historian Eric Goldman quipped, they "represent the kinds of effort too many lonely nights on the prairie give rise to." All writers must, however, come to grips with the problem of making what is said, readable. The injunction of the American Physical Society in their "Rules and Regulations for the Preparation of Abstracts" is well taken: "Make sure that what you send is easy to read, else some day you will get it back!" But while qualities of good report prose can be characterized by many adjectives—*accurate, precise, lucid, specific, factual, concise, objective, clearly worded, restrained, unambiguous*, etc.; to achieve a good, readable style poses difficulties for any number of persons.

Some are eternally confused between the polar extremes of conciseness and verbosity. Conciseness with reservation is, of course, a virtue. Quite often, lack of clarity results from the writer's uninhibited garrulity on the one hand, or his feeling for what the texts call "fine writing" on the other. The first type is like the preacher that David Harum, the upstate New Yorker in the 1899 Edward Noyes Westcott novel, found so unpalatable:

> ". . . it gen'ally seemed to me [said David] that if the preacher'd put all

the' was in it together he wouldn't need to have took only 'bout a quarter of the time; but what with scorin' fer a start, an' laggin' on the back stretch, and every now an' then breakin' to a stan'still, I gen'ally wanted to come down out o' the stand before the race was over. The's a good many fast quarter horses, but them that c'n keep it up for a full mile is scarce."

On the point of fine writing, a proneness to ponderous jargon results in a lack of clarity in many instances. When asked what his first deed would be if he were made Emperor of China, Confucius replied, "I would reestablish the precise meaning of words." One writer has said that our communication is getting lost in a "world of nonlanguage." We find ourselves often hammering on "interfibrous friction fasteners" instead of "nails"! We no longer put the family car on a grease rack for an oil change and motor tune-up; it now goes into the "lubridome" for a lubrication and "integrated engine analysis." We are lost in polysyllabic profundities. Words are not easily understood; they are unclear because the writer has not taken time to be considerate of his reader nor to acknowledge readability.

At the National Archives, that windowless building where I once worked, it has been found that the prose of the average Government agency runs a fog index of 26. "In other words," says their report, "you need ten years of post-graduate education to know what most Federal agencies are talking about." The Peace Corps is better than average—it has an index of only 23 (meaningless to the college graduate with the bachelor's degree). "The Pentagon reaches the outer limits," continues the report. "It has a 30 (unintelligible to the human mind)."

A 60-page report by Lawrence Klein of the Labor Department (1965) called Government writing "poorly done, murky, obscure, jargon-laden, awkward, dull, discursive and humorless."

This does not mean, of course, there is no place for technical vocabulary and its sometimes complicated expression. At times it is perfectly in order: the lawyer has to speak a language all his own, for the sake of legal precision; in his hands jargon becomes a highly codified, precise language, despite the fact that to the layman it seems quite abstruse. So, too, with what a geologist might say about "stable relict material, the plagioclase of basalt, altered to amphibolite by high temperature metamorphism, which may be retained and rimmed by actinolite in greenschists . . ." But there is no excuse for what one writer has called "a supreme piece of psychiatrese":

"... to treat patients by means of hormones, as insulin or adrenal cortical extract, or by means of carbon dioxide, is to attempt to improve the personality aberrations by altering the disturbed neuro-humeral integrative processes in the hierarchy at the relatively low degree of integrative complexity involving complex molecular configurations, and thus secondarily influencing the more complex integrative processes, and cause a healthier integration of the most complex integrative processes of personality."

If we Flesch this, says the writer, a sentence of no less than 73 words, simply bristling with affixes to the tune of 52, i.e., 71 per hundred words, confirms that this execrable prose is beyond the outermost pale.

And does any viable communication exist when a memo report states the following?

"The Technical Sub-Committee has evaluated plans for the initial study in what is anticipated will be a chain or sequence of pilot studies leading up to a major study in which several methods will be compared simultaneously."

It reminds me of what the Harvard historian said about Governor General Shirley of Revolutionary Massachusetts, that "he was always getting ready to begin"! One might have used the well known Buzz-Word Generator in the process.

Correct use of jargon is but one element in achieving satisfactory readability. The writer should learn to speak in essences, avoiding ponderous jargon but also not be long-winded by making too much use of weak words, and's and very's and is's. Combine elements, subordinate one idea to another to vary, strengthen, and shorten what must be said. J. Bennett Hill, of the Sun Oil Company, once cogently remarked at a Science Writers Conference in Philadelphia that "any full report, with effort on the author's part, can be boiled down to tell 90 per cent of the story with 25 per cent of the words." It's good advice.

Use the periodic sentence for emphasis. Give your reader a lift now and then by variety. Don't dangle elements, and don't be ambiguous. One who is concerned with communication effectiveness and clarity could do well to remember the story of the Genie who worked behind the soda fountain. When a customer said, "Make me a chocolate malted," the Genie did just that. And, like the customer who became a milkshake, writers cannot afford double meanings. When a metropolitan druggist advertised, "We dispense with accuracy" (there's one of the promotional double-meanings often met today), the druggist could get away with it, as can the local newspaper ad offering "Lady's Alterations," about which one editor quipped: "It does not say whether these are to be alterations made by a lady, or alterations worked upon a lady—we rather prefer the latter . . . (we'd make her) ten pounds thinner, a lot more patient, more interested in sports, (and) brighter in the morning(.)"

Eagle Shirts conducted a contest for new, creative color-names for their latest shirts. Among those listed in the final compiled report were gang *green*, navel *orange*, Freudian *gilt*, statutory *grape*, Willie *maize*, Dorian *gray*, and unforseeable *fuchsia*. In report writing we can't just call a spade a spade; it must be defined.

While ad-men draw upon ambiguity to attract readers and customers, the writer of straightforward informative prose—whether administrator, engineer, or report writer—must be careful to avoid it. He may feel he really belongs at the Bread Loaf Writers Conference, sitting at the feet of Howard Nemerov or Delmore Schwartz, but his responsibility is to leave the symbols and the plurisigns to the practicing poet.

Significant Aspects of Editorial Function

Proofread. A writer who has planned well and written with organization in mind still needs to check for the little things that can create serious problems in a finished document. The New Hampshire city report on the Administration's firm commitment to "the municipal work farce" was (we hope) just a typographical error. Remember Hamlet's "Let us couple Hell!" mispunctuated with a comma before the "Hell" makes a whale of a different imperative to Ophelia! You can have fun with any number of illustrations like these. The slogan of the International Paper, as you know, is "Send me a man who reads." One coed revised it to "Send me a man. Who reads?" Clarence Barnhart, editor of the Thorndike-Barnhart Dictionary, said he felt it almost impossible to avoid double meaning in English, though he thought he had one exception in "The fathers of our country were passionate believers in freedom." (Put a comma after the word *passionate*!) Some writers just sprinkle commas at random or mangle the English language unthinkingly—these illustrations simply point up the fact that proofreading is a must. Lack of correctness can make any piece of writing ineffective and the writer lose the respect of both his audience and his colleagues. In more practical terms, there may be times when it even loses contracts!

Use a style guide. Be sure, of course, that you have a good style manual or editor's and writer's deskbook. More than we sometimes like to admit, our dependence upon such tools is great. The American Institute of Physics goes so far as to assert that "This Manual will teach you how to replace the unprintable with the printable." A simple check at a glossary of usage would have made all the difference in the world in the RADC document that read

> "*Operating instructions*—These instructions shall be clear and simple. They shall be so complete that no verbal instructions are required."

And, believe it or not, one Army post memo said:

> "The Commandant objects to the use of the term 'verbal orders' when 'oral orders' is intended. He points out that verbal orders can be either written or oral since both employ verbs."

Check style: defuzz. There are those difficult areas where the writing may be technically inarguable, but the language still "sounds bad" and can be changed. A report which came to my desk contained this wording:

> If built, an IFF video processor should at least detect, integrate, range split, beam split, and degarble overlapping and interleaved IFF returns which are interlaced, and produce range, azimuth (or x-y), mode and code information once per target for all detected targets.

It sounded a bit like Samuel Johnson's classic definition of a *network* as "anything reticulated and decussated with equal distances between the interstices"! After some headscratching, we changed it to two sentences and an itemized listing:

> An IFF video processor should be designed to perform the following functions:
> 1. integration,
> 2. detection,
> 3. range-splitting,

4. beam-splitting, and

5. degarbling of interlaced IFF returns.

It should provide range, azimuth, mode, and code outputs once per target for all detected targets.

Now it was understandable, and presumably, clear to sponsor administrators also.

Check format. There is much more to editorial function than proofreading and defuzzing. Finally, one must take into account the overall document from style of writing to layout.

These four axiomatic rules of report writing are time-worn and also time-honored suggestions. One cannot fail to consider and to practice, however, the accepted standards of effective writing.

Yet, there is another point to report writing today, for these are the 1970's. Report writing, says the literature of the field in recent articles and reviews, has changed and is changing, but very little indeed has been pinpointed. In this Age of Technology, in this period of paper-work inundation and report proliferation, things *are* changing rapidly. "Out of complexity comes perplexity" might well be the maxim for the 1970's.

We need to ask ourselves relevant questions; to seek solutions to problems even before they arise as problems. This, after all, is what engineers, technologists, and social scientists have been striving to do—the people for whom and with whom we work. Why should not report writers try to anticipate the future requirements of their art?

- What will be the effect, for example, of increased alphanumeric character recognition (ANCR) employment, already in use by the postal service (address scanning) and Government report centers (reading of abstracts and digests)?

- What will be the effect of the whole acronymic craze? Is there a limit of reader toleration for acronyms in a report? How should they be handled for complete clarity and communicability to the reader? One engineer, in Bridgeport, Conn., has a favored sentence:

"The MTBF of MOSFET's, not including MWIC types, is based on the MTR derived on the figures supporting the SATYRR and PERT charts."

"That," he said "has everyone nodding agreement, as no one wants to admit ignorance." His satiric piece points up the problem of the widespread abuse of the acronym or initialism, however. He calls it UAP (Unintelligible Acronym Phraseology), and says the concept is invaluable in proposals, review and evaluation reports, progress reports, and other supportive software.

- Will we sacrifice style and grace for functional, technical syntactic coherence only?

- Will format become more standardized or will it become of so little importance that format diversity will be even greater than in the past?

- Will editing be done by computer? Will tech editors be replaced by some super-sophisticated rhetoric-computer version of the AFLE (automatic fault location equipment) that now doublechecks and troubleshoots military systems?

A recent item in *Computer Decisions*, one of the newest of publications, led off with:

> No fooling . . .
> No modifications . . .
> No misunderstandings,
> ComPutAmates Communicates.

Can we all say as much?

I don't know what the questions are, nor if these suggested are the essentially relevant ones for the 1970's. But I do know that in any gathering of writing specialists from diverse fields of industry, business, and government we at least have the opportunity to phrase a number of the questions. If there are none to raise, then I'd have to conclude the report writers' utopia must have arrived.

There's one further problem today relative to report writing; it is, essentially, the need to recognize that we have what the *Advanced Management Journal* calls "a paperwork Tower of Babel," in which our commonsense awareness of the functional value of document simplicity and directness is destroyed by complexity and sheer quantity. Birth control programs to curb the number of reports, for instance, are no solution; it simply can't be done. The need to write more and more reports increases startlingly with a seemingly geometric progression of study areas to be reported upon. We pile up memo after memo, report after report. Coming to grips with the problem of controlling the mass and magnitude is no small task. Within any installation, therefore, ground rules must operate to provide working procedures for investigation and reporting, as well as for administrative memoranda and correspondence. An executive administration that fails in this single area is inefficient and costly to the entire corporate entity.

A speaker from the University of Maryland once reminded a group of conferees that there are three maladies: writer's cramp, swelled head, and writer's itch. "The worst of writer's cramp," he said, "is that it is never cured; the worst of swelled head is that it never kills." But writer's itch is the commonest—and all of us have it to a degree, else we wouldn't be writers or editors of any kind. "Writing, if it be conscientiously undertaken," he concluded, with Baconian overtones, "maketh the exact man, which all men of science must be. [It] becomes deplorable only when it is pudderized into an *auctorial pruritus.*"

To quote again from Marianne Moore, from whom I drew the title for this paper,

> "A pleasing statement, anonymous friend.
> Certainly the means must not defeat the end."

Be lucid, be accurate, be succinctly informative. Above all, remember that all writing is meant to be read, hopefully, by other human beings. As long as we keep *that* in mind, report writing will remain an art, and human communication will continue to improve, whatever the state of technology.

CHAPTER 3

The Persuasive Proposal

DR. LOIS DEBAKEY
Professor of Scientific Communication
Baylor College of Medicine
Tulane University School of Medicine

"No man, but a blockhead," said Samuel Johnson, "ever wrote except for money." By that criterion, the grant applicant is no blockhead: he writes strictly for money. How can he minimize the likelihood of a rejection by the granting agency? There are safeguards, and many of them are inherent in the way he writes his application. Even those who deprecate a serious interest in language and writing as the concern of "pedants" recognize the utilitarian value of competent self-expression in a grant application. The ability to write persuasively, in fact, is crucial to a successful application, since it is the sole medium of communication available.

The retrenchment of research funds during the past few years has heightened the competition for grants. Gone are the days when research grants went begging. Only about 50 to 60 per cent of applications to the National Institutes of Health are now approved by the reviewing committees, and these applications must then survive a strict priority valuation before actually being funded.

We are all salesmen, whether we acknowledge it or not. Even though we do not make our livelihood selling automobiles, household appliances, food, clothing, real estate, advertisements, or other tangible products, effective salesmanship is the basis of most successful human endeavors. We are all daily involved in selling our appearances, our personalities, our characters, our talents, and our ideas. Certainly, the grant applicant is engaged in selling his ideas and his ability to carry out the activity described in his proposal.

Your goal as a grant applicant is to submit a *persuasive proposal*—one that convinces the reviewer(s) to approve the investment of the funds for which you are petitioning (Figure 1). You

Figure 1. The money man.

must, then, define yourself verbally as a good risk—as one who is capable of creative thinking, sound reasoning, and productive investigation. You may, indeed, be capable of all these things, but if you cannot, by the selection and arrangement of words on paper, convince the reader that you have these qualities, you may never receive the financial support necessary to demonstrate your skills, for most application referees judge the anticipated value of the proposed research on the basis of the care and precision with which the application was prepared. Careless words have often robbed applicants of the support they seek.

How can you enhance the persuasive force of your proposal? As in report writing, you will need to anticipate what your reading audience will expect from your application. If the sole evaluator is to be the director of your laboratory, you will write the application differently from one to be read by foundation reviewers who may have no special knowledge of the research methods you plan to use. Knowing your audience will help you decide what to include and how much to elaborate. You should therefore find out all you can about the agency or foundation to which you plan to apply: what its purpose and scope of research interests are, and how its applications are evaluated. Some grantors have special application forms, whereas others merely outline broadly what the application should include. Be sure that you have the latest guidelines and forms for applications, since obsolete information can lead you astray. The more you know about the grantor, its policies and purposes, the more likely you are to fulfill its criteria.

Naturally, you will want to select the most suitable agency for your field of interest. Most libraries contain a directory of granting foundations and agencies, with information about the scope of interest of each. The annual reports of agencies also usually list research projects being supported, but if these are not available, you may write directly to the grantor for descriptive information. Artificially adapting your purpose to satisfy the objectives of an agency will suggest a kind of intellectual dishonesty that will work against you.

Because the reviewing process for applications generally takes from six months to a year, you will be wise to begin writing your application well in advance of the projected date to begin the research. Plan on at least two months to prepare the application; anyone who has written a proposal recognizes the conservativeness of this estimate. Meeting the stated deadline is imperative.

Preparation of a grant proposal, an essential component of the investigator-educator's life today, need not be as painful as many applicants consider it. Yet even Nobelists like Szent-Gyorgyi [1] approach the task with distaste; grant applications, he admitted, agonized his entire scientific life. I am convinced that faulty methods used for instruction in language and logic are largely responsible for the anguish that most people experience when faced with the task of preparing a formal written or oral presentation. The dull, negative, impractical approach to English grammar and composition adopted by teachers in the early grades has produced

generations of verbally handicapped or inhibited graduates [2].
These inhibitions can, however, be released by the application of a
few basic principles of effective self-expression.

These principles apply equally to the preparation of a grant
proposal and to that of a scientific or technical report, despite
several differences in the two forms. The temporal relation between
the writing and the research, for example, differs. You write the
proposal before you know the results and the *report after* (Figure
2). The proposal is a forecast; the final report a retrospection. In

Application ➡ Grant ➡ Report

Figure 2. Temporal relations of grant application,
research project, and final report.

the proposal, you need to convince the evaluator that you have the
critical faculties to recognize a gap in knowledge or other need and
the creative imagination to devise a way of filling that gap or need.
The successful research applicant is the one who can reduce the
contradictions, the illogicalities, and the ambiguities in uncharted
regions to predictable phenomena expressed in simple, cogent
terms. When you write the final report, on the other hand, you
have the results before you and so can write factually rather than
anticipatorily. In both the application and the report, however,
you must persuade the reader that your thinking is clear and your
reasoning sound [2]. The difference in time of composition does
not, therefore, affect the essential criteria of composition:

Content	*Form*
Worthiness of subject	Clarity
Propriety for the reading audience	Conciseness
Clarity of purpose	Continuity
Accuracy	Transition
Unity of thesis	Consistency
Orderly organization	Simplicity
Coherent development	Readability

Preliminary Planning

A frequent, and grievous, error among novices is to begin writing
too soon. The result is a diffuse, rambling, confused proposal that
lays bare the incertitude and chaotic thinking of the applicant. An
obscurely defined, vaguely described, sloppily developed project is

bound to suggest murky thinking and is likely to portend haphazard research. Before you write the first word of the proposal, make sure that the concept you plan to examine has some point of originality, that it is well defined in your own mind, and that it is worthy of support. To satisfy these three criteria, you must have a good grasp of current knowledge on the subject, which means that your preliminary bibliographic research must have been thorough. If your application betrays an ignorance of certain vital aspects of the subject, you will be judged poorly qualified to perform the work, and the funds you seek will be refused. Writing down certain ideas as you go along in your preliminary planning often helps crystallize important points in your own mind. If you are later able to use some of this material in the proposal, so much the better.

When you have carefully delineated the purpose and scope of your study, have a good understanding of its relation to present knowledge on the subject, have planned your method of attack, and feel reasonably comfortable that it will yield desirable information, then and only then should you embark on your writing project.

PRELIMINARY AIDS

First, write down on paper the *precise question* or problem you plan to study. Make sure it is based on a sound premise. Then write the possible or *expected answer(s)* or solution(s). Seeing these two ends of your research project on paper will fix the limits of your study firmly in mind. Next write the *title*. Make it accurate, clear, succinct, and provocative. You will, of course, want to re-examine the title later, after you have completed the proposal, but writing it now will help circumscribe the subject in your mind. An informative title is indispensable; select key words carefully to highlight the essence of the subject. To abbreviate a long title, such as:

> Some Theoretical Foundations and Some Methodological Considerations for Thesaurus-Construction,

you can often use a broad main title, indicating the primary disciplinary category, followed by a more limiting subtitle, such as:

> Thesaurus-Construction: Theory and Method.

Titles such as the following cannot be expected to excite the reviewer:

> Investigations into Implicit Speech Inferred from Response Latencies in Same-Different Decisions.

Outline—With the question, the possible answers, and the title before you, and with the purposes and goals of the granting agency clearly in mind, prepare an outline of the proposal, to insure unity of thesis, completeness of content, orderly organization, and coherent development of ideas. Even if the granting agency provides a format for the application, you will still need to outline your material in order to develop your central thesis cogently. The outline is a skeleton or frame on which to build the proposal; you should use it as a guide, but be its master, not its slave. Feel free to modify it any time you recognize a deficiency or error in it. Because it is merely a preliminary design or pattern, it need not be excessively detailed; in fact, minutiae are often distracting and confusing. A sentence outline, however, is better than a jot outline because it requires you to organize your material in the same grammatical unit that you will use in the actual paper. Once you have made your outline, you can adapt it to any particular application format.

Synopsis—Next, write a synopsis of the proposal, in which you succinctly define the purpose, describe the methods of procedure and their rationale, summarize the expected new knowledge to be gained, and indicate its anticipated significance. The agency's guidelines usually specify the length of the summary, but rarely is more than one page necessary. Since most agencies require a summary of the proposal, the synopsis has a utilitarian purpose beyond encouraging conciseness and giving a bird's eye view of the proposal as a whole. You will, of course, need to re-examine the synopsis after you have completed your full proposal, but writing it at this point will help you put your ideas in proper focus and balance. Use of key terms in the summary will help the reader focus immediately on the salient features of the project. The synopsis should be comprehensible to the nonspecialist.

The Proposal

With the preliminary steps completed, you are ready to draft the proposal proper. Write the first draft with attention exclusively to orderly sequence and without consideration for grammatical or rhetorical perfection. Stopping to examine each word, phrase, or clause will shift your attention from thought to form and will interrupt the rational flow of ideas. You can always refine your composition later, but if the presentation of your ideas is disorderly, major excision and reconstruction will be required to repair the damage. Use succinct language and assign to appendices any auxiliary information, to prevent cluttering the text with excessive detail.

INTRODUCTION

In any unit of exposition, be it a sentence, a paragraph, or a full composition, two of the most important positions are the first and the last. The introduction, therefore, should be prepared with special care, for if you fail to engage the reviewer's interest in the beginning, you may lose it altogether. Take a lesson from the prosperous house-to-house salesman who attributed his phenomenal success to the first five words he uttered whenever a woman opened the door: "Miss, is your mother in?" That salesman recognized the importance to successful communication of knowing your audience and making your introduction attractive; he engaged the interest of his audience immediately, and he encouraged receptivity in his opening words.

Even if the reader is a reviewer who is compelled to proceed beyond a dull introduction, you risk putting him in an inhospitable mood. To avoid such nonreceptivity, make your introduction straightforward, sharp, and provocative. If you are long-winded in the beginning, the reader has reason to conclude that you are incapable of sweeping away the irrelevancies and the extraneous from the subject under consideration, and that you are not therefore likely to design and conduct an efficient, fruitful program of study. State the problem and the aims clearly and promptly rather than make the reader traverse several pages before he finds out what your central point is. Justify your study of the problem by putting it in perspective with respect to what is already known, including your own previous work on the subject, and explain how you plan to add to current knowledge. Emphasize what is unique about the project. State clearly the theoretic basis for the study if there is one, and indicate briefly how you propose to test the theory.

Your opening paragraph should inspire confidence and convince the reader that what you wish to do warrants careful consideration. Grants are made on a competitive basis, and the merit of your proposed study will be evaluated on the basis of the words you write in your application. If you fail this first test, you may forego the opportunity to explain further, or to defend, any statements which the reader questions or challenges. *Remember that cold print alone must sell your idea.*

MATERIALS AND METHODS

The introduction should lead naturally and smoothly to the section on methods, which is probably the most carefully examined section of the grant application, and therefore one of the most important. If it is superficial and poorly focused, you are not likely to receive approval. Your purpose here is not so much to allow the reader to duplicate your studies, as in a scientific report, but rather to justify the rationale of your study. Describe clearly the method of selection of subjects or materials and the provision of controls for variables that might later be confused with experimental effect. To defend your choice of procedure, you must obviously be familiar with the capabilities and limitations of all available methods. You will want to present alternatives in case your method of choice should prove unsuccessful or inadequate. A discursive presentation of all possible approaches, however, will indicate inadequate critical ability. You should anticipate and compensate for any weaknesses or defects in the method chosen, and should explain precautions to be taken against possible bias. Guard against selecting a sample that is too small to yield reliable results; a biostatistician can be of assistance in determining an adequate size for the sample. Describe also your proposed method of analyzing and interpreting the data, and indicate the anticipated time schedule for the project.

Be sure that your experimental design is rational, ethical, and defensible and that it can yield answers to your stated problem. When the proposed experimentation has ethical implications, it is wise to include a statement of approval of the research protocol from the responsible administrative authority in the parent institution.

Never assume that the reader knows anything of vital significance that you have omitted from your presentation. Even if he knows it, he will not know that *you* know it too unless you tell him. Make certain that you have at least described the sample, the experimental design and procedure, the method of collection and analysis of data, and the time schedule. Considerable time can be lost if the agency must request additional information before a decision can be made.

EXPECTED RESULTS

Following the section on methods is that on expected results, which should be written honestly and objectively. Overstated claims and unwarranted predictions of dramatic "breakthroughs" should be avoided in favor of sober statements based on logic and reason. Try to estimate the potential generality of the results and the basis for your judgment. When tables and graphs summarize data for this section more efficiently than text, they may be used to advantage. Any tests, instruments, publications, films, or other educational material that may be by-products of the project should be noted.

DISCUSSION

In the Discussion, you have an opportunity to show your broad familiarity with the various aspects and implications of the problem and to present the potential significance of the prospective results. Be sure to indicate any distinctive qualities of this research as compared with previous studies. Wild speculation is anathema. This is the place to persuade the reader that your proposed study holds real promise. You will also want to explain your method of assessing the results as a measure of the success of the project. And you may wish to suggest new directions for subsequent or concurrent projects in related research.

REFERENCES

References, instead of being listed at the end, as in a published report, are usually included in the text. Choosing references wisely will testify to your knowledge of the field and your skill in evaluating previous studies. If you omit a reference to previous work because it weakens your argument or shows your study not to be original, the reviewer will assume that you are not adequately informed in your field. A lengthy, uncritical list of references is equally bad. Painstaking accuracy in citing references reflects favorably on the reliability of the applicant.

PERSONNEL

Qualifications of applicant—In addition to the description of the proposed study, the applicant is expected to establish his ability to carry out the study by presenting his qualifications in the form of a curriculum vitae and to provide some evidence of his productivity by attaching a list of his publications.

Other personnel—Applications should, when possible, specify the names, titles, and qualifications of all personnel expected to participate in the project. Indicating the research experience of participants is also helpful. No one should be listed, of course, without his or her explicit permission. Consultants and research teams or agencies that have agreed to provide assistance and co-operation should be included.

FACILITIES

Indicate the space and facilities available for use in this project, including special facilities, such as computers and libraries. Additional space needed should be noted.

BUDGET

The budget should represent a careful estimate of the financial needs to conduct the study. Honesty and common sense are the best guides in preparing the budget. Your ability to direct the study efficiently will be judged partly by your acumen in estimating the costs.

Make certain that you have taken account of fringe benefits for all personnel, such as social security and insurance, and have included an item for overhead, when necessary. Consider whether you will need to pay for transportation of subjects, professional travel for personnel, statistical analyses, preparation or publication of reports, or similar items. Special large items of expense require textual justification. It is wise to have a business manager or purchasing agent review your budget before submission of the proposal.

TABLE OF CONTENTS

A table of contents is welcomed by most readers who wish to review the scope of the proposal before reading it or who, after having completed the first reading, wish to review certain parts of the application. It also serves the writer as another index of the completeness and orderliness of the organization of the proposal, as well as of its strengths and weaknesses. This page obviously cannot be prepared until the application is completed.

REVISION

When you have completed the first draft, lay it aside for a couple of weeks or so—long enough to be able to read it with detachment and objectivity. If you re-read it too soon, you may read what you *thought* you wrote, not what you actually put down on paper. Read first for logical order and coherence, accuracy, clarity of purpose, unity of thesis, and consistency; then for grammatical integrity, punctuation, grace of expression, and mellifluence [3]. Note, too, whether the narrative flows smoothly and logically from one statement to the next and from one paragraph to the next. Reading aloud will uncover defective rhythm or cadence, as well as improper balance and emphasis.

If I had to identify the most important literary requisite for grant applications, I would choose precision—precision in choice of words and in their arrangement to convey the intended meaning. Because our language often uses hyperbole and irony, it is tricky and requires considerably more care to convey meaning properly than most of us give it. For example, "fat chance!" actually refers to a slim chance, and "I could care less" means the same as I couldn't care less. Our language also has a certain amount of built-in ambiguity that results from the multiple meanings of certain words and of the different syntactic structures into which they can be placed. For this reason, the writer must be careful about involuntary double meanings, as exemplified in Figure 3.

The order of words in English is all-important because position contributes greatly to meaning. There is a vast difference between:

Have you anything left? *and* Have you left anything?

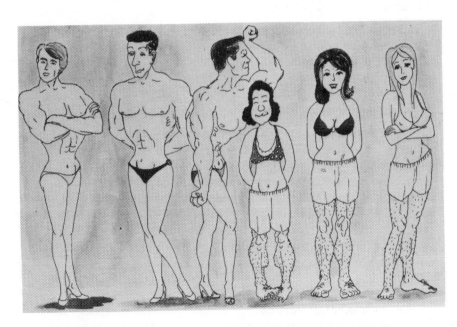

Figure 3. Ambiguity: The group was composed of half men and half women.

Misplacement of a single phrase can thus play havoc with meaning, as in the following:

> The patient would get chest pain *when she lay on her side for over a year.*
>
> Remedied: *For over a year* the patient would get chest pain when she lay on her side.

A dangling construction like this can also distort meaning:

> *At the age of six*, the patient's mother died of cancer.

Obviously, the patient's mother was not six when she died of cancer.

> Remedied: When the patient was six years old, her mother died of cancer.

Close behind precision as an important quality of grant applications is *conciseness.* Not that your composition should be telegraphic or cryptic; rather that you should weed out the pure verbiage, which irritates and bores the reader. You would be surprised how much you can tighten your prose by eliminating the common forms of wordiness. You can, for example, delete introductory deadwood like this without affecting your message in the least:

> It is interesting to note that,
> It should be pointed out that,
> It should be remembered that,
> It is significant that,
> It is worthy of note that,
> It has been demonstrated that.

All these expressions occupy valuable space and time without contributing to meaning. Draw a line through them, and capitalize the next word.

The shortest distance between two points, verbal or spatial, is a straight line, and the more unnecessary words you use to express a thought, the longer it will take your reader to grasp the idea. Look carefully, therefore, for facile but cumbersome circumlocution, and substitute for it the more efficient and more eloquent shorter phrase or word:

Circumlocutory	*Concise*
an excessive amount of	too much
at a high level of productivity	highly productive
at a rapid rate	rapidly

at no time	never
due to the fact that	because
has the capability of	can
in the majority of cases	usually
in close proximity to	near
in view of the fact that	since
it is the opinion of the author	I think
present a picture similar to	resemble
serves the function of being	is

Redundancy slips easily into writing because certain prefabricated expressions are so widely used that they come unbidden to mind. A careful rereading, however, will uncover such superfluity. The people who review your application were selected because of their sharp critical faculties, so you need not use phrases designed for the dimwitted, like:

ancillary aids
basic fundamental essentials (Three times, the charm?)
cause was due to, *or* reason was because
cut section
efferent outflow
green in color (As opposed to shape?)
human volunteer (Is there another kind?)
obviate the necessity of
period of time (As opposed to space?)
past memories (As opposed to future?)
psychogenic origin

Tattered phrases, too, impede communication. Exhausted from overuse, these expressions no longer function serviceably, but merely lull the captive reader into somnolence, which may continue throughout the rest of the application. Try, therefore, to root out meaningless banalities like:

a growing body of evidence
a thorough search of the
   literature
a large body of information
   (Figure 4)
an in-depth study
appears to be suggestive of the
   possibility that
beyond the scope of this study
by and large
crash program

few and far between
first and foremost
for all intents and purposes
in the final analysis
last but not least
longitudinal studies
matter of course
new avenues are being explored
suffice it to say
warrants further investigation

Figure 4. Cliché: A large body of information.

Some expressions recur so often as to have become absolutely sterile (see Figures 5, 6, and 7).

Imprecise, capricious language is often a serious impediment to communication [4]. Sprinkling your proposal with unnecessary jargon, as in the following sentence, will not ensure you a position in the inner circle, but rather will expose your lack of resourcefulness:

> Effectiveness on the output side of the management prong (information disseminists, documentalists) requires in-depth knowledge of input procedures, relevant sensitivity parameters, and the development of a high index of suspicion of surrogation probabilities.

Vogue words mark the copycat, and whereas they may add spark when first used, their vigor quickly withers from overuse. Moreover, the very evanescence of these terms makes them inappropriate for serious writing. Remove from your application, therefore, in-words and expressions like: ambience, at this point in time, conceptual framework, dialogue, hopefully, in terms of, input, interface, knowledgeable, meaningful, monolithic, relevant, seminal, simplistic, societal, surrogate, viable, visceral, vis-a-vis.

Figure 5. Cliché: The new treatment should prove to be a valuable addition to our therapeutic armamentarium (reproduced from DeBakey [6]).

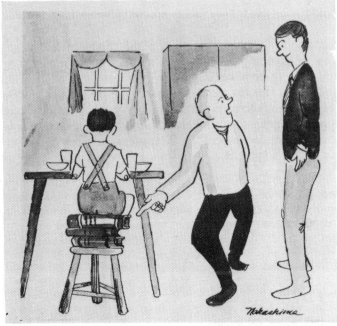

Figure 6. Cliché: This study fills an important gap (reproduced from DeBakey [6]).

Figure 7. Frozen expression: The monkey proved to be the most suitable model.

It is similarly unnecessary to impress the reader with your erudition by using pompous words, esoteric or abstruse phrases, or arcane terms. The discriminating reviewer is not awed or intimidated by such phrases as information data base, media method module, satellite preparation, target population, or learning activity package, nor does your promise of a sequential unit report move him to approbation. The reviewer will, in fact, either scratch his head perplexedly or silently hurl execrations at you if you write such spurious profundity as this:

> These perceptual processes are coupled with cognitive functions such as memory and logical thinking which enable adaptive modes of behavior to be deduced from the demands of internal and external reality. Whereas the expressive and defensive functions are sensitive to constancies and may steer the organism toward creating constancy, the adaptive function is oriented toward change.

Such language seems intended more to conceal than to clarify meaning. The reader will react more favorably if you stick to simple, natural, clear language.

Avoid the freshman's thesaurus-syndrome, in which long synonyms are substituted for simple words in the hope of making writing sound more erudite. This practice has functional hazards, since synonyms usually have at least shades of difference in meaning, and often may have one sense in one context but an entirely different sense in another context. After returning to his native country, a foreign student was writing a letter of appreciation to his American teacher. At the end he wanted to write, "May Heaven preserve you," but was not sure of the meaning of "preserve." First he consulted a dictionary and then a thesaurus and wound up writing, "May Heaven pickle you." Synonyms can trip up even native speakers that way.

Unvarying use of the passive voice, rather than reflecting objectivity, as some suppose, conveys a sense of uncertainty, defensive circumvention, or simple evasion. Rarely does the passive inspire confidence or induce positive action. Try, therefore, to turn around syntactic structures to allow the use of an active, vigorous verb. An accomplice of the passive voice is the abstract noun as subject, which, having emasculated the action, requires a weak verb to complete the thought. Note the difference between the following two sentences:

1. *Re-implantation* of the severed arm *was accomplished* by the surgeons.
2. The surgeons *re-implanted* the severed arm.

The visual image of the abstract *re-implantation* in (1) is weak by comparison with that evoked by the active verb *re-implanted*. Releasing the verb in the abstract noun in (1) produces the more forceful and more direct statement in (2).

By examining your proposal carefully with these common literary breaches in mind, you can improve the quality of your writing noticeably. Scrutinize every word, asking yourself if it is necessary to the meaning, if it is the precise word you need to convey your meaning, and if it is in the best position in the sentence to communicate that meaning [5, 6]. The more attention you give to these flaws, the more critical you become and the more sensitive to infelicities. The best way, incidentally, to acquire an ear for language is to read good writing—fiction, poetry, drama, prose— whatever you like, but *outside* your field of professional interest.

Critical Review by Others

When you have done the best you can with your proposal, give a clean, double-spaced photocopy to a respected critic who will not withhold constructive criticism for fear of injuring your feelings. Ask him to be ruthless and exacting, for you can be certain that the official reviewers will be just that. Omission of critical information or a flaw in structure may thus be uncovered. A fresh reader can also often point out blind spots that the writer is unaware he has. Inadvertent humor, for example, often escapes the author but is obtrusive to the eye of a new reader:

The foot on the other hand appeared swollen (Figure 8).

Figure 8. Inept figure of speech: The foot on the other hand appeared swollen.

This disputable statement occurred in a prestigious medical journal:

Autopsied men who ate more than 33 per cent of the experimental meals served from entry into the trial to death were more likely to have gallstones (Figure 9).

Authors, editors, and proofreaders all overlooked that incongruity.

Finally, let your laboratory director or departmental head review your application. Most grants today are made to institutions, not to individuals, and you will therefore probably need his approval and that of your institutional head. It is unfair to expect to rush your application through his and other administrative hands at the final hour; allow enough time for it to be processed in the routine way.

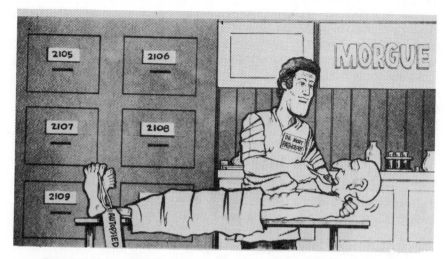

Figure 9. Autopsied men who ate more than 33% of the experimental meals. . . .

How Important Is the Actual Writing?

Is so much care really necessary in the preparation of an application? After all, you say, is it the applicant's literary proficiency that is under scrutiny or his ability to perform the proposed work? The answer is: both. Some believe, in fact, that the two are inextricably related, and that vague, obscure, disorderly writing reflects the same kind of thinking. Certainly, it seems reasonable to question how clearly a person has conceived his ideas if he is unable to convey them intelligibly. It seems equally reasonable to expect the person who submits a loose, sloppy, ineffectual application to conduct a loose, sloppy, ineffectual study. Moreover, since the utility and value of the results of the study depend on the applicant's ability to present a lucid, coherent report, a poorly written application may signify the writer's inability to communicate any new knowledge which his study uncovers. And the greatest of truths, poorly communicated, remains unconvincing. The history of science and technology is interspersed with valuable observations that were ignored or forgotten for years because the published reports were inscrutable or otherwise ineffectually presented.

APPEARANCE

The physical appearance of the proposal leaves a distinct impression on the reviewer. If the application is messy, illegible, or otherwise unattractive, the reviewer will be irritated or unreceptive even before he begins to read the proposal. Such nonverbal devices as punctuation, spacing, paragraphing, and underlining are valuable signaling tools that will help the reader understand the text more readily. Review the headings, marginal headings, paragraph headings, tables and graphs, and other such elements to make sure they are logical, consistent, and attractively arranged.

Criteria for Evaluation of Grant Proposals

The peer review system has served science and technology well. Referees usually serve without remuneration, giving generously of their time and effort for the general good. It is a mistake to consider them as adversaries, for their guidance, although not infallible, has generally proved sound in the judicious dispensing of limited funds.

Applications for grants are usually judged on the basis of the following criteria:

The Research Project
   Relevance of the research problem to the purpose of the agency
   Originality of the concept
   Importance of the problem; need for research
   Soundness of scientific rationale and approach
   Adequacy of experimental design and detail
   Feasibility of scope
   Appropriateness of budget to proposed work
   Suitability of facilities

The Investigator
   Education and training
   Experience
   Research competence
   Adequacy of knowledge of research field
   Promise
   Previous productivity

Before submitting a proposal for consideration, the grant applicant would do well to make sure that these criteria are fulfilled.

Summary and Conclusion

Retrenchment of research funds in recent years has heightened the competition for grants and has emphasized the importance of careful preparation of research proposals. Applying the principles of sound reasoning and clear expression will help the applicant fulfill the criteria of a persuasive proposal: a worthy concept for study, clarity of purpose and scope, and a scientifically valid design for the study, with adequate controls and appropriate method of evaluation—all expressed in orderly, coherent fashion and in simple, concise, readable prose. Thinking through the entire proposal clearly before beginning to write, composing the first draft with attention to logical sequence of ideas rather than grammatical perfection, and removing from the preliminary drafts certain common literary flaws are three steps that will surely enhance the persuasive quality of the proposal.

The applicant should remember that the proposal is a kind of promissory note. It is a mistake to promise mountains and deliver molehills, because the day of reckoning will come—when you will have to write a formal report of your research project. It is through writing, therefore, that both the need for the research and the importance of the results are communicated, and the investigator with literary prowess has a distinct advantage in achieving both of these objectives.

REFERENCES

1. A. Szent-Gyorgyi, Looking Back, *Perspect Biol Med, 15,* pp. 1-5, 1971.
2. L. DeBakey, Releasing Literary Inhibitions in Scientific Reporting, *Can Med Assoc J, 99,* pp. 360-367, 1968.
3. ____, Competent Medical Exposition: The Need and the Attainment, *Surgery, 60,* pp. 1001-1008, 1966.
4. ____, Verbal Eccentricities in Scientific Writing, *N. Engl J Med, 274,* pp. 437-439, 1966.
5. ____, Every Careless Word That Men Utter: I. The English Language, *Anesth Analg* (Cleve), *49,* pp. 567-574, 1970.
6. ____, Every Careless Word That Men Utter: II. The Language of Science, *Anesth Analg* (Cleve), *49,* pp. 827-832, 1970.

CHAPTER 4

Planning the Technical Paper

JAY R. GOULD
Professor of English
Rensselaer Polytechnic Institute
Troy, New York

The typical technical paper has many things in common with the typical report. As a matter of fact, the paper is often derived from a report, particularly a research report.

When you go to an engineering conference and listen to the papers read, you can easily see the various stages through which the material has gone. First has come the report, probably an internal report from the researcher at the laboratory to his supervisor or to other interested people.

Then along comes word of a conference and the researcher decides to present his findings through the presentation of a paper. Sometimes the paper is published directly in the *Proceedings* of the conference. And sometimes it undergoes minor changes and appears in a journal.

The Abstract

Most journal papers begin with an *abstract*. Very often limitations of length will be placed upon you by the editor and you will be asked to submit an abstract of a certain length. Naturally, the length is determined to some extent by the length of the paper itself.

The form of the abstract is largely determined by the use to which it will be put. If it is a *descriptive abstract*, it may do little more than tell what the unifying idea is, and in the most general terms. This kind of abstract is useful only for indexing purposes and for retrieval purposes. Here is an example of a *descriptive abstract*:

This paper describes integrated-circuit content-addressable memory designs employing simple memory cells that are compatible with peripheral circuits designed for existing I C random-access memories. Operating algorithms of the proposed content-addressable memory are also discussed.

This type of abstract tells the busy reader that he will have to read the paper clear through if he is to get the information.

For most purposes, the *informative abstract* is much more useful. Not only does it describe the project in general terms, it also describes the project in specific terms. How much more useful is the abstract illustrated here:

Collector—diffusion—isolated (CDI) device structures offer simplified processing and increased circuit packing density, and result in competitive electrical performance characteristics. The direct application of CDI to transistor-transistor logic (TTL) circuits designed for conventional integrated bipolar devices, however, results in degradation of certain circuit performance characteristics. It is demonstrated here that optimization of the TTL circuit configuration and CDI component design results in circuit performance levels that at least equal those achieved with conventional bipolar structures, while maintaining the packing density and simpler processing advantages of CDI.

A family of beam-lead sealed-junction CDI-TTL circuits has been designed and fabricated. The CDI-TTL gates comprising these circuits have a typical propagation delay of 4.0 ns at fan-out of 1, average power dissipation of 6 m W, and a worst case noise margin in excess of 200 m V over the temperature range 0-90°C and fan-out 1-8.

Introduction

Just as in the report, the paper will probably start with a section called *Introduction*. This will include the reason for writing the paper (purpose), how much ground it will cover (scope), and will usually contain the unifying idea. It may also deal with the historical background of the project, fundamental theories on which the research has been based, and any other information needed by the reader before he gets into the new material.

Conclusions

This matter of conclusions is quite typical of the technical paper and the report from which it is often derived.

By placing *Conclusions* in the *Introduction*, or at least early in the paper, the reader can quickly determine the principal features of the paper. He does not have to wade through the conclusions for himself.

Sometimes, however, the conclusions are placed at the end of the paper. Here is an example in which they do little more than repeat the material already in the *Introduction*:

The high-frequency characteristics exhibited by the MESFET prove the usefulness of field-effect transistors for microwave applications. The amplifier described here is but a first step. An amplifier and osculator development program is continuing. Our goals are to develop broad-band devices capable of operation through X band.

A much more satisfactory conclusion section can be found in a paper on a transistor. In this example, the author summarizes what he has already described—his results and conclusions. He then goes on to show how this research can be applied.

It has been shown that a recessed-gate structure can also be used in the case of an enhancement MOS transistor. The advantages are higher stability and higher gain in the high-frequency region. A drastic reduction of the reverse transconductance (by a factor of 8-12 at 1 G A_Z) can be reached; the increase in gain is about 3.

Because the distance between the gate edge and the drain is very critical, a careful alignment procedure is needed.

The new element presented can be used for fast switching applications and high-frequency linear circuits. To realize the good high-frequency behavior, packaging must be avoided. In future experiments, the entire circuit will be integrated in the same substrate.

Procedure

Once the *Introduction* has established the purposes of the paper and its limits, and the *Conclusions* may or may not have been provided, the technical paper is likely to backtrack.

A section is now provided that returns to a chronological order to tell the reader how the writer went about his project and his experimentation. This section is usually called *Procedure*. Its contents will vary with the demands of the project itself.

The *Procedure* section of any technical paper may be comparatively complicated. It is analogous to the researcher in his laboratory getting ready to work. He must find the space for his experiments, decide on the material he will use, and set up apparatus to carry out his project. He will then begin the experimentation. And this is what the procedures section of the technical paper does.

A paper in the *Journal of the Optical Society of America* uses a section titled *Experimental Procedure*. A few sentences from this will indicate how the authors followed up the introduction.

> The experimental arrangement is shown in Figure 1. The laser beam is focused into a sample cell with a long-focal-length lens, and illuminates a small column F of the sample through a 0.35-mm-diam pinhole.

Experimental Procedure in this paper then is followed by a section on *Experimental Details* and a section on *Experimental Results*.

Sometimes it is necessary to include the procedures section information on materials, apparatus, and personnel. These three items are particularly important when the research being done has little precedent, both in the ideas presented and in the procedure itself.

In the journal *Steroids*, it is fairly common to find a section or sections on *Materials* and *Methods* as indicated in this short excerpt.

Materials and Methods

> *Reagents.* All organic solvents were purified and redistilled according to standard procedures.
> *Buffer Solutions.* Krebs Ringer bicarbonate with 0.2% glucose (KRBG). Phosphate buffer pH 7.6.

Another paper from the same journal follows the same plan:

Materials and Methods

> *Radioactive compounds.* All the radioactive steroids used in the present experiments were obtained from New England Nuclear, Boston, U. S. A., and purified before use by paper chromatography.
> *Reagents and solvents.* All carrier steroids were recrystallized. Reagents and solvents used were of analytical grade.

After the description on materials and methods, the usual practice is to follow through with the main section on procedure, as we have already indicated.

One element often found under *Procedure* is *Description of Methods.* Here is an opportunity to describe the basic nature of the study and to give the reader the way things were carried out before he is given the *Results.*

Description

Sometimes the description is an important, integral part of the procedure. Descriptions usually break down into three categories: descriptions of machines, processes or operations, and theories.

It is difficult to imagine a procedure that doesn't involve a machine or a mechanical device of some kind. Sometimes the description can be very brief; at other times, it must be extended, especially if something new is being offered the reader. These guiding principles should help you.

1. Tell what the machine does and why it is important to the study as a whole.
2. If the machine is in any way unusual, say so and show why.
3. Describe the machine in broad, general terms before you take up details.

An excerpt goes like this:

In general, an associative processor excels at searching through rapidly changing lists of random digital data for a desired item at perhaps 1,000 times the speed of the conventional computer. It also excels at performing arithmetic operations on many pairs of numbers, with a speed advantage of perhaps 300.

The associative processor's basic building block is a 256-word module. It contains 256 processing elements, each consisting of one response store and its length of plated wire, and 256 interrogation drivers, each driving a printed-circuit conductor, or "strap."

A description of a process or an operation may be the principal part of the paper. But sometimes it is only a small part of the procedure.

The process can be described in a manner similar to the machine.

1. The reader must be told at the beginning what the end product of the process is.
2. If the process is new and different, this should be included as well.
3. Very often materials and machines are integral to the process.
4. A general description should be given before detailed steps are included.

The following excerpt illustrates a brief description of a process used in connection with a water treatment plant.

In the past decade technical advances in water treatment equipment have been made and the two leading processes developed are *electrodialysis* (ED) and *reverse osmosis* (RO). Test and failure data show the ED unit to be superior in performance and reliability.

Electrodialysis is a process using electrodes and semi-permeable membranes that permit the passage of either cations or anions.

The basic unit is the cell-pair consisting of a cation and an anion membrane separated by a spacer for guiding the liquid flow. Many cell-pairs are combined to form a "stack" which includes two electrodes connected to a direct current source.

When current is applied across the stack, the positive ions move in the direction of the cathode and negatively charged ions move toward the anode.

The description of a theory, or an idea, or a principle follows the same general technique as for the other two types.

1. The importance and uniqueness of the theory is given.
2. The importance of the theory is stressed and any practical application it may have.
3. Then the theory may be described in its historical context.
4. Finally, details are described.

This excerpt is taken from an electronics magazine:

In 1962 Brian Josephson, a graduate student at Cambridge University, made some startling predictions. He said that if two superconductors were weakly coupled, a dc current would flow between them without any potential being applied. He also said that a bias applied across the superconductors would generate an ac current with frequency proportional to the bias level.

The dc Josephson effect refers to the ability of a junction to generate a current in the absence of an applied voltage. The externally induced ac Josephson effect refers to the fact that, when a junction is irradiated by a signal of frequency f_s, its I-V curve takes on the appearance of a staircase. The internally induced ac Josephson effect refers to the generation of an ac current by Vo.

After ten years, Josephson junctions are beginning to leave the laboratory and enter the real world. This summer The National Bureau of Standards will begin using them as the primary voltage standard for the U. S. In medical research, they are measuring magnetic fields from the heart and the brain. IBM and Bell Telephone Laboratories are studying their usefulness for computers.

Results

Then comes the section on *Results*, probably the most important part of the paper. It is impossible to lay down any kind of hard and fast rule on how this section should be written up because it depends entirely on how the experimentation has been carried out and the results may therefore be quite unpredictable.

Discussion

Following *Results* is usually a section on *Discussion.* Many editors tell us that this section is frequently the most difficult to whip into shape because it is inclined to be subjective, diffuse, and full of opinions.

Some Typical Outlines

Outlines for writing the technical paper will be useful only if they can be adapted to the material you present. On the other hand, most journals do request their contributors to follow certain general outlines. This is not difficult to do as the paper is far more restrictive in presentation than the article. It has been derived from methods of research that have been perfected in laboratories for decades, even centuries. The readers of the paper are authors in reverse; therefore they understand the procedures of research and expect to find the written paper follow pre-determined formulas.

Here are a few outlines of papers taken from well known journals.

From the IBM *Journal of Research and Development* comes this classic outline:

    ABSTRACT
    INTRODUCTION
    EXPERIMENTS
        Materials
        Apparatus
        Procedure
    RESULTS
    DISCUSSION
    ACKNOWLEDGMENT
    REFERENCES AND NOTES

From *Steroids* comes this outline:

    ABSTRACT
    INTRODUCTION
    MATERIALS AND METHODS
    RESULTS

DISCUSSION
ACKNOWLEDGMENT
REFERENCES

From the *Journal of the American Oil Chemists' Society*:

ABSTRACT
INTRODUCTION
MATERIALS AND METHODS
RESULTS AND DISCUSSION
REFERENCES

Aids to the Paper

Although each paper is different from any other, there are still aids and techniques that are common to all, at least within a particular discipline.

BIBLIOGRAPHY

Most technical papers carry a section on bibliography. Sometimes it is labeled *bibliography*, sometimes *references*.

The reason for including a bibliography is two-fold: 1) it attests to the authenticity and the reliability of the research being described; 2) it serves as a means for the reader to expand further his knowledge of a particular subject.

The position of the bibliography may vary from journal to journal. In most cases, however, it appears at the end of the paper.

The form of the bibliography also varies from one group of publications to another. The only way that you can be sure of the form to use is to read through some back issues of the journal. The most obvious place to look is at the ends of the papers.

Frequently, however, the journal itself specifies its own form. The IEEE *Journal of Solid-State Circuits* contains this statement in *Information for Authors*:

References may appear as numbered footnotes or in a separate bibliography at the end of the paper. In either case, references should be complete and in IEEE style:

Style for papers: author (with initials first), title, journal title, volume number, month, year, inclusive page numbers.

Style for books: author, title, location, publisher, year, page or chapter number (if desired).

Here are samples from this journal:

F. M. Smits and E. K. Sittig, "Ultrasonic digital storage, present and future," *Ultrasonics*, Vol. 7, 1969, pp. 167-170.

E. R. Chenette, "Noise in semiconductors devices," in *Advances in Electronics*, Vol. 23, L. Martin, ed., New York: Academic Press, 1967.

The American Mathematic Monthly makes this statement: "Please use the *Manual for Monthly Authors* (Vol. 78, p. 1) and follow the format in current issues of the *Monthly.*"

These are references from this journal:

Bush, Vannevar, 1960. Science; The Endless Frontier. National Science Foundation, Washington, D.C.

MacLane, Saunders: Hamiltoman Mechanics and Geometry, this Monthly, Vol. 77 (1970), 570-586.

If you are in doubt about the bibliographical form, the required information is usually given in this order:

Books
Author; Title; Place of Publication; Publisher; Date
Papers
Author; Title of Article; Name of Journal; Volume Number, Date of Issue (or both); Pages Used.

Whatever bibliographical form you use, be sure that you use it consistently for any one paper.

FOOTNOTES

Authors frequently are at a loss as to how much footnoting they should use. Several suggestions will help you.

1. Information that you could find in several sources usually is not footnoted.
2. One or two footnotes will be sufficient for blocks of ideas that you have cited from other sources.
3. Specific facts, not found in reference books and other general sources, should be credited to individual sources. There should be a footnote for each source.

As methods of using footnotes are discussed in every standard style book, it seems unnecessary to go into the subject in detail here. As with most mechanical devices used in writing, consult the two most authoritative sources: 1) standard reference books and 2) the style manual for the particular journal you're writing for. If the journal does not put out a style manual or it is unavailable, get your information by looking over several issues of the journal.

ABBREVIATIONS

In technical papers, abbreviated forms of technical terms are frequently used in the main text as well as in the references and footnotes.

But the system of abbreviating will depend largely on you and the journal. It would be foolish to say that all journals use the same system. However, more and more of them are depending on the American National Standard Institute's *Abbreviations and Engineering Terms*.

The most difficult decisions on abbreviations must be used in the text itself. About all we can say is, use them sparingly. On the other hand, it is impractical to write out *centimeter* every time; use *cm* instead. Omit periods unless the abbreviation spells a word, as *in.* for *inches*. Use the same abbreviations for the plural as for the singular.

A sentence from one journal reads:

> Jet engine turbine discs at 18kg (40 lb), grinding wheels at 23 kg (50 lb), and electric motors at 45 kg (100 lb) are now skinpacked.

A sample of a couple of reference items from another journal is almost unintelligible, except to people in the same field:

> Aman, E. 1966. The relationship between human and animal trains. *Trans. Roy. Soc. Trap. Med. Hyg.* 60.
> Dodes, R. 1957. Biology and pathogenicity of cattle. *Am. J. Vet. Res.* 16.

HEADINGS

It's the rare journal that doesn't break up the text by means of headings. This practice serves several purposes:

1. Headings make the text easier to read. They break it up and create a feeling that the information is being given in workable units.
2. Headings can be used by the reader as a means of referring to a specific section in the paper.
3. Headings, especially in journal papers, help the reader to identify the various parts. He will know where to find the *results* or the *procedure* or the *materials*.

4. Headings help the writer to produce a unified piece of writing. He can transfer many of the items in his outline to the paper itself, thereby maintaining a unity that he has predetermined.

On the whole, the technical paper is not as difficult to organize and prepare as the technical article. On the other hand, the paper must exhibit unusual accuracy; it usually records the results of original research and it is often used as an intermediate step to more research.

CHAPTER 5

Effective Oral Presentation of Scientific and Technical Information

DR. HERMAN A. ESTRIN
Department of Humanities

DR. EDWARD J. MONAHAN
Department of Civil Engineering
New Jersey Institute of Technology

Effective Speaking

When we look at successful men, we find that the single trait they share is an ability to use words effectively. How did they acquire this ability? How can *you* acquire this ability? You need *exposure* and *practice* to speak well before a group.

PREPARING FOR THE TALK

In preparing for a talk, you should first determine the restrictions. Ask about the following:

1. The length of the talk.
2. The setting of the talk, particularly those factors which could restrict your choices in planning the talk. Two extremes are:
   a. The podium setting: a fixed microphone and large audience.
   b. The flexible setting: small audience or lapel microphone, and the probable use of some forms of visual aids.
3. The use and the availability of visual aids.

Next, consider your audience. Its size will affect your possible choice and preparation of visual aids; its sophistication will dictate the technicality of your talk.

Now, ask yourself:

1. What notes should I prepare? for a podium talk? for other settings?
2. What visual aids are desirable? How do I use them effectively?
3. Should I rehearse?

THE USE OF NOTES

As with extremes of settings, there are corresponding extremes in the forms your notes might take. In the podium setting, where movement is not easy, you may be tempted to read your paper. Unless there are compelling reasons (e.g., an exact time limit), *Don't!* It is the rare person who *ever* learns to read papers well, especially highly technical papers. First, concurrent reading and thinking are difficult. (How many times have you heard a person inadvertently read from one sentence into another, or misread a word which of certainty is part of his vocabulary?) Second, the speed of reading is usually such that taking notes is virtually impossible. Third, if the paper is to be published, or will be otherwise available, the audience can read the paper at its leisure. Why should anyone want to hear you read it?

Topical outlines. Some experts, notably many educators, advocate the use of detailed topical outlines, with attention to various topics being timed to the minute. We do not recommend this technique, largely because spontaneity is not possible; the whole presentation will often seem "canned" and lifeless.

Key word notes. We do recommend a *key word* form of notes—the shorter, the better. The key words should be used to establish the *sequence* of topics. When you are completing one phase of the talk, you need merely glance at the notes (if necessary) to *stimulate thinking* about transition to the next topic. If the talk has been prepared well, such transitions should be natural. Do not commit the notes to memory. The timing of such talks is difficult for the beginner, and you will need much practice in your early efforts. Private run-throughs or partial run-throughs are suggested. Or you can try the technique in situations where there are no time restrictions. In time you will gain confidence in the method.

REHEARSAL

Rehearsals may help you fix the priority of topics more firmly. Then, if the talk is running long, the topics of lesser priority may be omitted to insure emphasis on the major points of the talk. If your talk is running short, there are two alternatives: devote more time to questions, or stretch the talk by interesting relevant digressions. Get your material for digressions from extensive but casual *peripheral* study of your subject, especially from sources other than those which are strictly technical, such as newspapers, news magazines, TV (documentaries), and especially current best sellers. Almost all technological problems have scientific (ecological) and sociological connotations which may not be germane to the technicalities of your subject, but which would be nonetheless of considerable interest to your audience. Your effort in compiling such peripheral knowledge should be minor and well worth the confidence you will gain.

Nervousness is normal to the beginner. But if your preparation of both technical and peripheral material is extensive, the temptation to read your paper or to prepare extensive notes can be overcome. With exposure and practice, the nervousness will surely subside.

It is unlikely that the vitally necessary exposure will be gained unless you make special efforts. Following are some suggestions:

1. Join or form a toastmasters' club.

2. Get a group together, find an empty classroom, and "have at it"; review each other's efforts.

3. Ask questions and supply comments at meetings, in class, and at lunch. Do so with a conscious effort toward the improvement of clarity of expression, diction, spontaneity, and enthusiasm.

Visual Aids

Assuming that the setting of your talk permits a wide choice, use visual aids such as:

1. The chalkboard
2. Poster, charts, maps
3. Standard projection equipment:
   a. Movie projector
   b. Slide and filmstrip projector
   c. Opaque projector
   d. Overhead (transparency) projector
4. Models, prototypes
5. Flip charts
6. Unique or novel devices

The following are our suggestions for the effective use of these visual aids:

THE CHALKBOARD

Plan *key sketches* carefully. These are the two or three sketches (graphs, plans, profiles) which illustrate the most important points of your talk. Additional board work may be necessary and even desirable to amplify explanations of the key sketches or to respond to specific questions. If considerable board space is available, place the key sketch conspicuously in the center and move to the sides for supplementary work.

Discuss or explain the material *as you are doing the drawing.* This technique will take much practice, but there are no really effective alternatives.

Bear down on the chalk! Lines should be strong and lettering should be large and neat. Aside from legibility and neatness, don't overlook the psychological impact of assurance on yourself *and* on your audience. Write with élan!

Be sure that your audience knows what you are drawing. Indicate PLAN, or PROFILE, or SECTION A-A, and ask your audience if they understand the orientation. You can usually tell by their reaction; a nodding head (eyes open!), an expression of interest.

Mark the ordinate and abscissa of every graph clearly: AXIAL FORCE, P, TONS; rather than "P." Indicate on all maps such items as the north arrow and street names.

POSTERS, CHARTS OR MAPS

When the material you wish to present is too complex for the effective use of the chalkboard, prepare or obtain a poster, chart, or map. (1) Be sure that such a visual aid can be seen by a person in the most remote section of the room. Test it yourself. (2) Plan for minor mechanical details. For example, is the chart stiff enough for propping? Is there a place for propping? Will thumbtacks or masking tape be needed? Watch out for rolled-up posters; they have a way of wanting to stay rolled (a manifestation of The Theory of the Perversity of Inanimate Objects).

Don't let a visual aid become a disaster!

STANDARD PROJECTION EQUIPMENT

You may wish to consider electromechanical equipment such as the movie projector, the slide and filmstrip projector, and the overhead (transparency) projector. The effectiveness of such aids will be influenced greatly by the amount of your *personal involvement* in the preparation of the projected material.

1. Use personal slides.
2. Prepare overhead transparencies and overlays. Use a felt pen to add notes during the talk. (Overlays are excellent visual aids; they allow you to "build" a complex drawing by stacking transparent component parts.)
3. Be cautious of the use of purchased slide sets, sound films, narrated filmstrips, and opaque projectors. These *may* be used effectively, but there is a danger of substituting the device for *personal* projection. If such aids are adopted, careful study is necessary. Avoid extensive use of the opaque projector.
4. Familiarize yourself with the use of the equipment. Make sure that it is working! Attend to details such as checking for outlets, extension cords, darkening the room (and reading your notes, if any).

MODELS, PROTOTYPES

Audiences respond with great interest to the display of hardware. Museums and libraries will often lend such material without cost. Or you can make a model. You may also wish to consider demonstrating testing equipment.

FLIP CHARTS

These may be effective, but care must be taken to avoid over-dependency. Otherwise an overly programmed talk may result.

UNIQUE OR NOVEL DEVICES

Use your imagination! Novel visual aids flatter your audience, gain their attention, and stimulate your own efforts at developing an interesting talk.

An excellent example of novelty was a student's use of a cloth board and cloth "pasties" in a talk on "Beach Erosion and Protection on the New Jersey Shore." He illustrated wind directions, wave and current directions, sand movements, and various types of shore structures by the simple but clever use of colored cloth geometric shapes which were placed on a large cloth board. The effect was excellent.

Delivering the Talk

The elements of delivery may be listed as:

- *Voice*, including projection (strength), diction, enthusiasm, tone variations, speed
- *Movements*
- *Gestures*
- *Eye Contact*
- *General Technique*, a broad classification including important intangibles such as attitude toward audience (formal, informal; serious, humorous, pompous, unaffected; etc.)

We present this list in the sense that it is virtually impossible to change one element of delivery without affecting most of the others. Think about this list! If you consciously improve the quality of projection, would not the elements of diction, enthusiasm, tone variations, and speed improve *naturally*? Try projecting without good diction, without enthusiasm, without tone variations, or without slowing down your delivery. Try standing still. Hold your arms and hands limply at your sides and stare at the floor while you *project*. You cannot! So improvement is not nearly as difficult as you might surmise.

With this totality of the elements of delivery in mind, let's consider some details of each item.

VOICE

Projection. This requires conscious effort, especially during the seconds *preceding* the start of your talk. Have you ever seen a weightlifter "psych" himself preparatory to a lift? In a similar way, you should take a deep breath and (figuratively) let out a shout (heeahh!) at your audience. *And project!* Keep the fellow in the last row in mind. If you suspect your projection is weak, ask a friend to sit in that last row and have him coach you with hand signals.

Enunciation. Enunciation is frequently a problem brought about by early environment, by carelessness, or by a combination of these factors. Thus, we say "Where ya goin?", rather than "Where are you going?" The slurring or omission of the "ing" endings is probably the most common diction error. We suggest two remedies. First, analyze your *conversation*, or (better) ask a good friend to alert you to your diction errors, especially the glaring ones of great frequency. Second, work to eliminate such errors from your conversation. The emphasis on conversation is important, since habit (i.e., carelessness) is in large part responsible for poor diction.

Animated delivery. Enthusiasm and tone variations are important. You cannot expect your audience to react positively to a monotonous, sing-song presentation. Be natural. "It was an arch dam," and "Two thousand people were killed within six minutes by the overtopping of the dam," are statements which deserve widely different deliveries.

Pausing. Speed of delivery, pausing, and repetition are affected mostly by the type of notes which you prepare. Other factors include your knowledgeability of subject matter, nervousness, and your geographic background (extremes: urban New Jersey and rural Oklahoma). As already noted, if your notes are extensive, you will be tempted to read or rely too heavily on the notes; to do so will thereby result in too rapid a delivery.

If, on the other hand, you have the conscientiousness to research your material thoroughly and the courage to prepare only key word notes, your problems at first will center around pausing and repetition, which are related. When the words do not flow freely, you will be tempted to fill the pauses with "ahs." Many other beginners favor, "Now . . . ," used repeatedly. (And, of course, once in a while you encounter experts: "Now, ah . . .")

To cure the pause-repetition syndrome, consider the following devices:

- During pauses (which, incidentally, we consider necessary and desirable), say nothing! But appear thoughtful, calm, and non-committal. It is not an easy technique, and it will require great restraint to resist the "ah" instinct, but it is most effective when it is done properly. (The master at such delivery was Douglas MacArthur.)
- Develop pause-filling phrases, i.e., *substitutes* for the "ah" and the "now" and the "now, ah." But be sure to vary the phrases so as to avoid excessive repetition of the substitute! Suggestions: "Let's think about that . . . (pause)." (Here you *tell* the audience that you are pausing.) "That is an excellent question . . . any suggestions?" (Here you are stalling by passing the buck to your audience temporarily.)

What do you do if you have prepared a key note talk, if you forget your place, and if you are ten feet from the podium—a common nightmare? Two suggestions: first, you may rely on the thoughtful pause approach while you are strolling to the podium; second, you may wish to loosen your audience up with a little humor by an exaggerated tip-toeing to the podium. (I once saw a math professor do this, with the remark, "When I first started teaching, this used to embarrass me; now the only thing that bothers me is missing those short putts." The effect was excellent.) An alternate to either of the above techniques is to carry your notes *inconspicuously* (but *only* key word notes, perhaps on 3 X 5 cards).

Colloquialisms. Use slang and colloquial expressions infrequently and only with careful thought about the effect. Project your personality but consider the sensitivities of your audience. Many students in the technological academic setting are at an age when the pressures to "be one of the guys" are still felt. Thus, there results such phrasing—these are actual quotes—as, "The water zonked down to here," and "Imagine a poor slob . . ." It is clear that such phrasing is more influenced by habit and by peer pressure than by mature reflection on effective speaking.

MOVEMENTS

You should be aware of the effect that movement has on your-self and on your audience. Certainly there is something more relaxing and informal about a talk in which you move away from the podium. Such movements are easy and natural when you use visual aids. Conversely, an overdependency on copious notes tends to anchor you to the podium and results in the development of a formal, dull presentation, delivered at too rapid a pace.

GESTURES

We can make a distinction between minor gesturing (mostly the hands, arms, and head) and major gesturing (where major body movements are involved). The distinction is made because the former types are mostly governed by habit and thus can often be distracting to an audience—even annoying. (The chin-jutting finger-poker is an especially annoying species!)

Should you employ gestures at all? We recommend that you do. But we turn once again to the concept of the totality of the elements of delivery to offer our recommendation: that the minor gesturing accompany voice projection and movement. Be natural. When you walk, your arms swing. When you then speak of something dynamic, the voice and hands will rise naturally and in harmony. Your eyes may widen and you may turn from your walk to suddenly confront your audience. You are being expressive!

How about major gestures? We recommend that you plan these, but only if the subject matter warrants the treatment. Such gestures should be broad, almost pantomime. Indeed, they should be considered as novel visual aids. Suppose, for example, that you are discussing dilatancy of a saturated clay soil which is being subjected to shear forces. You wish to emphasize the fact that negative (vacuum) pore-water pressure will develop and thus result temporarily in increased shear resistance. Everyone in the audience will have shovelled slush. Make reference to this, grab a "shovel," dig in, and pantomime the motion of shove-and-(quick) lift. At this point a widening of the eyes and an exaggerated swallow will be natural and minor gestures which will help to make your point effectively about temporary increases in shear strength in such situations. (It will also guarantee a laugh.)

EYE CONTACT

Be sure that you direct your remarks and your eyes to all parts of your audience. Above all, talk to people rather than to windows, floors, or podiums!

Evaluation

COMMON ERRORS

We present here our listing of common deficiencies observed in new speakers and suggest that you analyze your own efforts to determine whether you have similar problems. The listing is a summary of notes made during talks by about 300 junior and senior civil engineering students. Order of listing is about the order of frequency.

- Poor board work, diminishing in quality as the talk progressed.
- Lack of movement; overuse of notes. These errors are related. Commonly, the student would sit at the desk with a thick sheaf of notes, frequently losing his place. The reluctance to move was, it is thought, based upon his attachment to the notes.
- Monotonous voice.
- Lack of enthusiasm.
- Poor eye contact.
- Repetition of certain phrases: "The next thing is . . . ," "Now . . ." (By actual count, ten times in 80 seconds!)
- Careless enunciation common to New Jersey, "gonna."
- Overly colloquial language; slang: "Imagine a poor slob . . . ," "Water *zonked* down to here . . ."

Identify your weak and strong points by self-critique. Write an appraisal. You might rate yourself on each of the elements of delivery discussed in the preceding section. (Outstanding, Excellent, Very Good, Good, Fair, Poor, Very Poor) Now the moment of truth: have others make the same appraisal! Compare notes. (You may be surprised; we are, constantly!)

Evaluate the effectiveness of visual aids by asking specific questions, for example:

1. Was my board work clear and was it explained clearly? Especially the key sketches?
2. How about supplementary board work?
3. Did I speak too fast?

IMPROVEMENT OF VOCABULARY

Prepare, deliver, evaluate, improve.
And so it goes. The improvement will come with exposure and

practice, but your improvement will be dramatic if you make a conscious effort between talks.

We specifically recommend the following:

Dictionaries. Buy *several* good dictionaries for places where they will be handy: your office, your study, your stand near the T.V. lounge chair, perhaps (a small one) for your briefcase.

If you are the type of person who can write down a new word or in some other way remember to "look it up later," you can save some money. (But we can't! Can you?)

Light reading. Analyze your *nontechnical* reading (news, sports, novels, etc.). How often do you encounter a new word (so that you can use those expensive new dictionaries?). If the answer is "seldom," you might consider other sources of light reading. After all, such reading need not be inimical to self-improvement. To be specific, *Sports Illustrated* is an excellent source for vocabulary development for beginners.

Games and puzzles. Look for word games or "tests" which are published regularly, crossword puzzles, for example. *The Reader's Digest* has a regular feature, "It Pays To Increase Your Word Power," which we recommend. (Not incidentally, we heartily concur with the title.)

Patience. As a general recommendation, we would suggest that your efforts toward vocabulary improvement should be steady and conscious. Avoid crash programs which tend to become chores and thus often short lived. Be patient. When you find a new word, look it up, and study the context in which it was used. Don't use it in speech until you have seen or heard it used several times, perhaps in various contexts. Soon it will be "yours"—painlessly.

FOR IMPROVEMENT OF DELIVERY

Speaking technique is a very personal trait. With this in mind, we offer the following suggestions. Some you may find useful; others may be contrary to your personality. Above all else, be natural.

1. Observe others for technique. Avoid their errors and consider adopting their strong points. Watch for interesting phrasing, but avoid overuse (e.g., "In my judgment . . ."). Especially

watch, listen, and study the good and the great: Movies: Richard Burton, Lawrence Olivier; World politics: Abba Eban; Records: Winston Churchill, Douglas MacArthur; Sports: Curt Gowdy.

2. Adopt some humor if at all appropriate. Learn a few good audience-relaxing stories. Beware of long jokes!

3. Develop methods of eliciting audience response. Ask questions. Poll your audience on questions which may have interesting statistical answers.

4. Make complimentary reference to personal friends who are present.

5. If you *must* read your paper or use extensive outlines, use a lectern. There is something indefinably awkward about such a talk without one.

6. Avoid . . .
   - "snow jobs"
   - affectations (especially overenunciation)
   - pomposity
   - verbosity

PART THREE
Technical
Communication
in
Practice

CHAPTER 6

Producing Good Technical Communications Requires Two Types of Editing

E. F. BOOMHOWER

Systems Development Division
International Business Machines Corporation
Research Triangle Park, North Carolina

To most people, the word "editor" usually connotes a literary editor. However, preparing technical documents requires two types of editing. These two types cannot be clearly and completely separated. But the primary and lesser responsibilities of each type can be defined. Such a definition can make it easier to divide responsibilities if both types of editors work on a technical document. It can also serve as a checklist to prevent overlooking any responsibility if one editor is performing a dual role.

Types of Editors

The *literary editor* is sometimes referred to as a copy editor or, perhaps, production editor. The other type of editor can be called the *technical editor*. Both types are concerned that a technical document conveys its message as clearly and concisely as possible. But each emphasizes different aspects of technical exposition in trying to achieve this clarity and conciseness, and readability and usability. In general, we could say that the *literary editor* is principally concerned with the mechanics of writing and producing a document, while the *technical editor* is principally concerned with technical content and the techniques of developing good technical exposition.

LITERARY EDITOR

The literary editor's responsibilities. In sorting the various aspects of editing, we may find it simpler to first define the aspects of primary concern to the literary editor. The literary editor is intimately concerned with:

1. Correctness of grammar, punctuation, format, style, and the like.
2. Good usage of the language.
3. Sentence and paragraph structure.
4. Use of capitalization and punctuation and various typographical devices to properly assist in placing appropriate emphasis and subordination.
5. Format and style consistencies such as treatment of figure captions and heading levels.
6. Other details such as spelling and proofreading and proper layout.
7. All the various other things involving the mechanics of writing and production.

The literary editor is not primarily concerned with the technical content of a document, nor whether its organization is best for the intended audience. He is not primarily concerned that the document is technically complete and free from unnecessary technical details for the intended reader. And he does not necessarily possess any particular knowledge of the technical subject being presented, although he should possess some general familiarity with the terminology used to describe the subject.

TECHNICAL EDITOR

The technical editor's responsibilities. These things that are not of primary concern to the literary editor become of primary concern to the technical editor. Conversely, the things of primary concern to the literary editor are of secondary concern to the technical editor. This is not to say that the good technical editor shouldn't be adept at manipulating the language and style and format to properly express and emphasize or subordinate the ideas being presented. He must know how to avoid grammatical fuzziness that could lead the reader to misinterpret the technical message. But, in general, the technical editor's contribution to the document comes at an earlier and more technical level.

The technical editor should have a general familiarity with the technical subject being presented, and should be thoroughly familiar with the technical terminology used to describe it. But, to maintain his ability to *represent the reader*, he should not be as familiar with the details of the technical subject as the technical writer is. He judges the manuscript on the basis of whether it tells him, in his *reader's* role, what he (the reader) needs to know . . . and only what he needs to know . . . completely, concisely, clearly, and accurately. In other words, he should be able to learn the technical details from what the writer has written; he should not know too much about the subject details beforehand lest he become unable "to see the forest for the trees." At every step along the way of manuscript development, this reader-representation aspect is probably the most significant contribution of the technical editor.

To effectively *play the role of the reader*, the technical editor concentrates on various aspects of the technical document. He works with the technical writer throughout the development of the manuscript to help ensure proper reader orientation and service. From the planning to the final manuscript stages he is concerned with the document's organization and flow, with its content and how it is presented. He asks questions like the following:

1. Does the writer have a workable outline that will enable him to achieve the appropriate content and organization?
2. Is there perhaps some trouble because the writer has not clearly defined the reader, in his own mind or in the preface material or both?
3. Is the material presented in the most useful order for the reader?
4. Is all the essential material included?
5. Is the message uncluttered by unessential information?
6. Are the transitions from topic to topic technically sensible and logical?
7. Are text and art effectively and properly coordinated to best present the technical facts and concepts?

8. Does everything that is presented really serve the reader, as opposed to displaying the knowledge of the writer?
9. Are the technical facts and concepts properly emphasized and subordinated in relationship to each other . . . neither attaching undue significance to minor points nor burying major points?
10. Is the general tone of the language used appropriate? For example, is the personalized or imperative tone used as it should be for instructional-type exposition?
11. In the final manuscript, are references and cross-references correct and sufficiently precise? For example, does every text reference call out the right illustration at the right time? And is every reference to other sections or books sufficiently explicit, not requiring the reader to jump around in tracking down information he needs?
12. Does the book require an index? If so, does the index do the job for the reader?
13. Are all the other elements that the reader needs present? These may include such things as: list of abbreviations; definitions of terms, in running text or in a glossary or both; table of contents to an appropriate head level; list of illustrations; how-to-use-the-book information; appropriate overall introduction and individual section introductions; appropriate safety section or notices; appropriate flagging of limitations and restrictions, in the index and otherwise; appropriate clarification of options available to the user; appropriate identification of hard facts versus opinions and recommendations; and absence of ethical and legal implications.

The technical editor cannot wait until the final manuscript is prepared to ask all these questions. He cannot effectively and completely play his role unless he begins working with the writer almost as soon as the writer is assigned the job. At an early stage he and the writer must agree on a definition of the intended audience and the level of knowledge of that audience. And he must help the writer develop a working outline that will serve that audience, and that will help the writer gather and sort out the appropriate technical details. Without this early and continuing writer/editor consultation, it is difficult, if not impossible, to achieve an effective, reader-oriented final document.

Another primary responsibility of the technical editor is to develop writers into better writers. This responsibility is at least as important as any other in producing quality documents.

Table 1 summarizes the aspects of editing and indicates the relative concern of each to the technical editor and to the literary editor.

Table 1. Aspects of Concern to the Technical and the Literary Editor

Editing Aspect	Relative concern[a] to	
	Technical Editor	Literary Editor
Correctness of grammar	2	1
Correctness of punctuation	3	1
Correctness of format and style	2	1
Good usage of the language	2	1
Sentence and paragraph structure	2	1
Literary pace and flow and transitions	2	1
Proper use of capitalization and other devices to achieve emphasis and subordination	3	1
Typographical and graphical consistencies	3	1
Spellings, abbreviations, etc.	2	1
Proofreading	3	1
Proper layout	2	1
Agreement with appropriate publishing specifications	2	1
Other miscellany involving mechanics of writing and production	3	1
Organization and flow	1	2
Working outline	1	4
Audience definition	1	2
Completeness of technical content	1	3
Conciseness of technical content	1	3
Correctness of technical content	1	4
Absence of unnecessary technical clutter	1	3
Familiarity with technical terminology	1	2
General knowledge of technical subject	1	3
Early and continuing consultation with writer	1	4
Technically sensible and logical transitions from topic to topic	1	2
Effective graphic techniques	1	1
Effective text and art coordination	1	2
Absence of bombastic displays of technical knowledge	1	3
General tone of language—e.g., personalized and imperative where appropriate	1	1
Clear, precise references and cross-references	1	1
Index content and serviceability	1	3
Appropriate preface and how-to-use information	1	2
Presence of appropriate other elements as needed—abbr. list, glossary, contents, illustrations list, safety notices, restrictions, facts vs opinions, etc.	1	1
Good introductory sections	1	2

[a] Relative weights: 1—of primary concern
2—of secondary concern
3—of incidental concern
4—of little or no concern or responsibility

CHAPTER 7

Making Technical Writing Easier

L. CLINTON HAWES

Systems Development Division
International Business Machines Corporation
Research Triangle Park, North Carolina

Since man first started scratching on cave walls, few effortless phrases have been written. Whether valentine couplets or pleas for money, they have usually been written, read, rewritten, reread, polished—even as these last two sentences have been. Irvin S. Cobb described his own writing something like dashing his stuff off madly at an inch an hour, using drops of perspiration for punctuation. He was speaking for most of us.

Writing, however, is not as difficult as many people try to make it. Poets and novelists may have to wait for an internal voice, but not technical writers. All writing is at least partly an art, requiring a degree of intellectual and emotional involvement. However, there are techniques which can be used almost routinely to make writing less mysterious and more repeatable.

Some of the "shortcuts" described in this article seem almost too simple to require elaboration; they are unfamiliar, however, to most programmers and engineers. Six techniques are discussed:

- Set up a "documentation" file for every potential project as soon as possible
- Take notes as soon as possible after ideas occur
- Fill in omissions by asking questions
- Underline key words and phrases in collected material and notes
- Use different types of outlines
- Treat the introduction as a separate task

Set Up a "Documentation" File for Every Potential Project as Soon as Possible

This seems an obvious first step in any writing project; yet how many technical people think about presenting papers or publishing when a project is initiated? By the time they do, several months, or years, later, valuable source material has probably been lost. Since any technical project of any worth will have something written about it—somewhere, some time—a file should be opened to collect raw materials for use in a proposal, report, memo, patent application, professional paper, or magazine article. Into the file goes anything remotely connected with the subject which might contribute to documenting it: memos sent and received, specifications, diagrams, proposals, reports, papers, and articles by you or others. Each level of communication can contribute to succeeding ones: memos to proposals, technical notes to reports, reports to papers, etc.

The secret is to start the file with the project, before valuable material has been misplaced, not with a publication effort. Professional writers keep many files open at a time, sometimes for years, which continue to grow until the time comes along when they can be used.

One of the most important additions to the file should be the inclusion of your own random ideas and comments—about the project or about what others have said about it. These can suggest or become a part of future documents; which leads us to technique number two.

Take Notes as Soon as Possible After Ideas Occur

Who hasn't tried in vain to recall a name, only to have it reappear later when it was no longer needed? Or had a brilliant idea while in the shower, which vanished on arrival at the office? Writers understand the importance and fickleness of the subconscious, and use special precautions to capture the elusive products of the mind. This concern is extended even to phrases and single words. It is much easier to jot down an apt word before it gets away than to laboriously try to dig it out of a thesaurus later.

The simplest solution is to carry a pocket notebook. When an idea strikes, get it down! When the ideas start coming, they are sometimes hard to turn off. Yet, we all know that the hardest way to turn them on is with a blank sheet of paper on the office desk. Use a separate sheet for each subject and write on only one side. The pages can then be torn out, taped or stapled to 8 1/2 × 11 sheets, and put in their respective files. If you collect enough ideas which can be pieced together, you may discover that you have almost authored a paper, with little pain. How to succeed in writing without hardly trying!

For more interesting ideas on writing in installments, see Herbert Michaelson, *The Incremental Method of Writing Engineering Papers.*[1]

Fill in Omissions by Asking Questions

Regardless of how much material you have collected, there will always be gaps which need filling in. These may be things which you know but just have never thought to put down. However, this step is more important if you need to use materials from others. Go over your source material, and again over your first draft, looking for these gaps. Abbreviations may have to be spelled out, terms defined. The additional information can usually be penciled into margins or on the backs of pages. Questions which often must be asked are:

- To what extent?
- Why?
- What is technologically new?
- How is the approach or technique different than those previously used?
- What are the advantages to the user?

Here are some examples of statements which lead to questions:

- "The circuit performed very well and gave the expected results." How well? What results?

- "An advantage of this circuit is the fact that its dynamic range is limited only by the stray capacitance of the circuit." What is the range usually limited by? Why is this circuit different? What's the advantage?
- "The speed is limited by the mechanical design of the terminal rather than by the transmission system." Why? Limited how much?

As you go through your source material, whether originally written by you or others, you may have additions, exceptions, or other comments. [To distinguish these, I usually bracket them.]

Underline Key Words and Phrases in Collected Material and Notes

You have collected a considerable quantity of notes and other material for your writing project. How can you untangle and remember it all? Your mind is better at organizing than the most versatile computer, but there are some things which you can do to assist it. One is used by almost every college student: underline key words and phrases which can be easily picked out and reviewed. This eliminates many of the connecting and filler words which constitute the bulk of writing. The results are similar to condensing material by taking notes, but much faster. (See Figure 1.)

What do you underline? Key and "flag" words and phrases. The

Read Only Storage (ROS) technologies play a significant role as major control elements in many of today's digital computers. Typically, the ROS is used to store microprograms which have been written by the computer manufacturer to perform diverse control functions within the computer—e.g., to interpret and execute programs in core storage written in the basic machine language of the processor.

The basic controls for the unit are provided by microprograms, but with one important difference—the microprograms are stored in a reserved portion of the processor's high-speed writeable core storage rather than in a separate ROS unit. This is significant not only because of the cost savings, but also because the microprogram storage is readily changeable, adaptable and reloadable and thus provides added capabilities in terms of improved serviceability facilities and increased configuration flexibility.

Figure 1. Underlining key and "flag" elements.

key elements are usually the most important nouns and/or verbs in a paragraph. Flag elements are those which point to key elements which follow. Examples are *one important difference, significant because, basic parameters, advantages, following reasons, first,* etc. It may be helpful to use different colors for key and flag words and phrases. A passage meriting special attention can be indicated by an "X" in the margin. Scattered references to the same subject can be tied together by marginal notes such as "See A, p. 23," etc. When information is organized at a higher level, it becomes less unwieldy. This is why we have such things as mathematical symbols and higher programming languages.

Use Different Types of Outlines

The engineer or programmer can use outlines in different ways, throughout a writing project. In addition to helping him plan his writing—the traditional role of outlines—he can use a *Writing Outline* to organize source material and guide the actual writing. Such use is a substitute for using note cards, with much less effort. More on this technique later.

The first type of outline which you may need is a *Review Outline* of a source document—a report, first draft, etc. (See Figure 2.) The outline enables you to quickly review both its content and organization. You need not worry about numbers and letters, but can indicate proper subordination by indenting. You should include all the headings used in the original document, plus subtopics. This is especially important if the headings in the source are inadequate or improperly located. The subordinate topics should be distinguished from the original headings in some manner, such as by underlining the original headings.

The Review Outline of a source may help you construct your *Planning Outline*—the customary outline of your proposed document. If you are having difficulty outlining your report, paper, or article, the *Master Outline* shown in Figure 3 may help get you started, particularly if it's hardware oriented. The headings are not the actual ones which will be used but guideposts; however, they include most of the categories which will be needed. No report, paper, or article will use them all. However, since most technical documents must be organized similarly if they are to be organized logically, most of the headings in your outline should replace or be a subdivision of one of the headings shown.

Since introductions are difficult to write—and outline—they are discussed separately, in the next section. If you are unable to

Introduction
    Purpose of integrated attachments
    Purpose of the Integrated Communication Attachment
"Writeable" Control Storage
    Comparison with Read-Only Storage
System/360 Model 25 Data Flow
    Core storage
    Auxiliary storage
    Local storage
    Arithmetic-logic unit
Priority of System Operations
ICA Overview
    Purpose
    Flexibility
    Number of lines
    Location
    Functional description
ICA Common Control
    Purpose
    Scanner operation
    Asynchronous selection of data adapter
    Types of microprogram traps
    Servicing priorities

Figure 2. Part of an outline of a source document. Headings actually used are underlined.

finish your outline, this—as well as the writing—will become easier if you progress to a *Writing Outline.* Actually, this is not a separate outline but an extension of the Planning Outline which you have been working on. It is obtained by keying your material and notes to the outline.

The first step is to read through your material and notes, numbering and giving a heading to each separate topic. (See Figure 4.) Next, code each document containing source material with one or two letters. Now go through the material again and transfer the document codes and heading numbers in the material to the headings in the outline with which the headings in the material seem most logically associated. (See Figure 5.) If you are unsure where a heading belongs, tentatively place its number (with document code) under more than one heading in the outline, as long as you don't have to do too many this way. If you have subjects which seem pertinent but do not fit anywhere, you may need to create more headings in the outline. Gradually, you are shaping a large, unwieldy mass of material to fit into your outline—and your outline to fit your material.

When writing, you need review only those parts of the material whose numbers are listed next to a particular heading in the outline. The *Writing Outline* is *dynamic*. New material or additional thoughts can be easily added while writing as long as they don't belong in a part already written. Some of the references will reference similar ideas; you can combine the best from all sources, or use them as cues to write something different. If ideas or facts don't seem to fit where you originally placed them, drop them down in the outline to a heading where they seem to fit better. At the same time, scan ahead to see if any material needs to be moved up in the outline. As you use material, cross the

---

Introduction
Historical Background
Analysis of the Need/Problem
Disadvantages of Other Solutions
Designing the Device/System
Device/System Description
    General--based on block diagram
    Detailed
Device/System Operation/Data Flow
Device/System Testing
Results (How well the device/system solves
  the problem/need)
Applications
Programming
How to Operate the Device/System
Summary
Conclusions
Future Use

Figure 3. *Master Outline.* Headings are meant to suggest categories, not headings to be actually used in finished writing. Not all of them will be used at any one time. The most commonly used headings are underlined.

Notes (N)

① Need

General need to reduce number of boxes
1. Saves cost
2. Saves space
3. Serviceability

Report (R)

① Common Control

The main element in the common control is a scanner which sequentially scans . . . once per machine cycle (900 nanoseconds), the scanner steps . . .

Smith's draft (S)

⑤ Common Control

The common control provides the interface between the microprograms and the data adapters. Its primary functions are to . . .

Figure 4. Excerpts from three source documents, showing codings and headings to be referenced in a *Writing Outline*.

references to it off the outline. Some of the material will be discarded and crossed off as soon as you come to it. If a heading has too many references to review conveniently, make a suboutline. As you review the material, you may see how you can improve on outline headings. (Many of these will not be used, or will be reworded, in the finished manuscript.) As you use *Writing Outlines*, you will grow in proficiency.

Treat the Introduction
as a Separate Task

The deficiencies of the following introduction should be obvious. "Consider a trapezoidal beam, $X C Y D$, rotated 37 1/2° clockwise from the perpendicular."

The introduction to almost any writing merits special consideration, for several reasons. It is the most difficult part because several things must be done at once within a very few words. The reader's eye may have been caught momentarily by the title or opening sentence, but his interest will probably be brief unless you can give him some additional reasons, very soon, for reading on. The introduction is the most important part of a report, paper, or article, because unless you *do* interest the reader, the rest of it will probably never be read.

To say that you must *interest the reader* is a gross understatement. You've got to clobber him! It may help to picture the typical reader: flipping through pages, with a stack of back reading piled up, much of it "required," and a strategy report to write, but wishing he could prune his prize roses instead, and wondering

---

Introduction	N7, R13, B8
System Operation	
General	P2, R30, N5, N21, A11
Data Paths	P14, R6, N17
Priority Levels	A6, R18, R20
Common Control	R1, S5
Data Adapters	
Start/Stop Adapters	T12, N3, N11, R19, A4, A5
Synchronous Data Adapters	S4, S16,
Autocall Adapters	A7, A8, N13, R5, R10
Microprograms	T2, V21, A9
Future Use/Evolution	R15, N16

Figure 5. *Planning Outline,* being converted into a typical *Writing Outline.* The references to headings in source material in Figure 4 are underlined. The other references are only for illustration. Comparing the *Writing Outline* to the *Master Outline* (Figure 3), note that three major headings—Common Control, Data Adapters, and Microprograms—have been substituted for *Device/System Description.* Also, because the material on *System Operation* was general and brief, this was placed ahead of the description of the system. The example illustrates how the *Master Outline* is meant to only suggest headings, not serve as an actual outline.

what the weekend weather will be like, and if he'll get his *Golf Digest* read before the next one comes. The only reason he's scanning your report or article at all is that someone put it in his pile and he'd hate to miss something he might be expected to know.

At the same time that you're trying to convince the reader not to pass up your contribution to enduring scientific literature, you've got to make a few introductions and these, as all introductions, are inherently dull. What is your subject? What kind of a report, paper, or article is it? You may want to refer to your organization or to why a device or technology was developed. Some of these should be woven in so they won't sound like answers to unasked questions. Reports and papers can have more formal introductions detailing what is to follow, mathematical background assumed, etc. However, this approach is rarely suitable for technical articles. One author wrote an introduction to an article which went something like this:

> "If you have even an elementary knowledge of communications, you will find this article too basic."

Limiting readership is not one of the usual objectives of magazine editors! Besides, who is qualified to prejudge the inclinations of all writers who might read a magazine, or to define something as vague as *an elementary knowledge.* Some things, even when true, are better left unsaid.

Most important, you must, early in your introduction, mention the advantages of your approach, implying that the reader may also enjoy them if he reads further and follows your example. Is it any wonder that writing an introduction is a challenge!

The intent is not to frighten you so that you'll never try to write another introduction but to impress upon you the loving care they deserve, and to suggest some approaches.

So, the first thing that you can do to improve your introductions is, perhaps, to change your attitude toward them. An introduction is not just a couple of sentences to "get you going," but a separate task, the most difficult and important in any writing assignment. You must expect to spend a lot of time on introductions, to rewrite them several times. They will seem easier when you realize that they nearly always contain the same elements: a sentence or two to attract attention and briefly introduce the subject, a description of the problem or need, the advantage to your way of solving the problem (the reason the reader should continue reading), perhaps more introductions.

The introduction may also include such elements as background to the problem, reasons for the unsuitability of other approaches, etc., if they do not rate more than a sentence or two. The body doesn't start until you come to a group of related ideas sufficiently extensive to merit its own heading: *Analysis of the Problem, System Description*, etc. If the report, paper, or article is extremely short, it may not have headings. The best way to learn to write introductions is to analyze several already published. It may be easier for you to write them after the rest has been written. But whether they are written first or last, they should be treated as an important, separate task.

Using these writing techniques is no guarantee that an engineer or programmer will be able to write deathless prose, but he who uses them will probably write more than he otherwise would have. He may even be spared a few of those beads of perspiration.

ANNOTATED BIBLIOGRAPHY

1. Bernstein, Theodore M., *The Careful Writer*. New York: Athenum, 1965.
   Advice on word usage and pitfalls from a bulletin circulated to reporters and editors of *The New York Times* since 1951, and two books which evolved (*Watch Your Language* and *More Language That Needs Watching*). The author is assistant managing editor of the *Times*. Perceptive, sometimes humorous, but not for the casual or occasional writer.

2. Gehman, Richard, *How to Write and Sell Magazine Articles*. New York: Harper and Brothers, 1959.
   A collection of articles with "How-to-do-it" introductions and "how-it-was-done" postscripts. Not addressed specifically to technical writers but of value to all article writers.

3. Gunther, Max, *Writing the Modern Magazine Article*. Boston: The Writer, Inc., 1968.
   Similar to Gehman's book except with fewer examples and more advice and anecdotes. Enjoyable reading.

4. Michaelson, Herbert, "The Incremental Method of Writing Engineering Papers," *Proceedings of the Society of Technical Writers and Publishers*, 1966, Paper No. 67.
   A novel approach to the perennial problem of getting technical people to write.

5. Mitchell, John H., *Writing for Professional and Technical Journals*. New York: John Wiley and Sons, 1968.

   The writing is as scholarly as the subject, with chapters on the organization of technical data, bibliographic procedures, and copious sample style guides and articles.

6. Rathbone, Robert R., *Communicating Technical Information*. Reading, Massachusetts: Addison-Wesley Publishing Company, 1967.

   A paperback which, in 100 pages, takes a refreshing approach to such perennial problems as the *wayward thesis, ubiquitous noise,* and *neglected pace.* Sub-title: "A Guide to Current Uses and Abuses in Scientific and Engineering Writing."

7. Strunk, Jr., William, and E. B. White, *The Elements of Style*. New York: The Macmillan Company, 1959.

   A lot of good advice on writing packed into a small paperback of 70 pages. The only book on grammar and usage that has ever made the best seller list.

8. Ulman, Jr., Joseph N., and J. R. Gould, *Technical Reporting*. New York: Holt, Rinehart and Winston, 1962.

   A well-known textbook on technical writing based on material used in MIT and RPI classes.

9. Weisbord, Marvin (editor), *A Treasury of Tips for Writers*. Cincinnati: Writer's Digest, 1965.

   A compilation of suggestions from 86 professional magazine writers, on almost every subject related to writing—from managing your time to using a tape recorder. A distillation of a wealth of experience.

REFERENCE

1. Proceedings of the Society of Technical Writers and Publishers, 1966, Paper No. 67.

CHAPTER 8

An Editor's Viewpoint On Preparing News Releases

SYDNEY F. SHAPIRO
Managing Editor
Computer Design *Magazine*

Introduction

The true measures of the success of a news release are how many times and where it gets into print. A consistently high level of success can result only when the information supplied is of interest to the readers of particular publications. However, a limiting factor is the manner in which the release is prepared. The most newsworthy item might be ignored if the presentation to the editors is poor.

Although not intended to be a text on the preparation of news releases, this discussion does point out key do's and don'ts—as viewed from the editor's side of the desk. The publicity writer who follows these points can be assured that his releases will at least receive better than average attention; after that, the outcome rests on the value of the information itself.

Preparing Your Release

Have a message! If you don't have something worthwhile to say, don't waste your time (and money) and the editor's time sending a release. There are always more than enough valid releases for an editor to use. Only a fraction can even be considered.

Before starting to write, decide why your release is worthwhile. Why should it be written? Who cares—other than your boss? If the release does not provide information that will be read and published, don't bother to send it. Usually news releases fit into one or more of several categories: product, news, developments, literature, personnel, corporate, and financial. Although some seem similar, each requires specific treatment. For best results, don't serve more than one purpose in one release.

Gather your information carefully and thoroughly. Get copies of all internal reports, eliminating all proprietary or confidential data. Talk to the key personnel involved until you thoroughly understand the project—not necessarily in all technical aspects, but at least so that you can verbally discuss the concepts intelligently. (Some editor might call you for more information or clarification of details.) Be certain you can back up all statements, either personally or through another company contact.

Follow basic reporting rules in writing the release (who, what, where, when, how), and make the release long enough to be useful. Provide both a short title (2-3 words) and a suggested caption (8-10 words) which abstracts the release. Place the title about one-third down from the top of the page and add the caption between the title and the first paragraph of the release.

Once you have determined the purpose of your release, summarize your story in the first paragraph. (Some editors will use only that paragraph.) Be certain the product is specifically and correctly named here and that its function is clear. After the summary, add paragraphs in order of importance. (The editor will probably cut from the last paragraph forward.) Give pertinent facts, and give enough to tell the full story. Give sufficient information to prevent misinterpretation; don't exaggerate. Be clear and precise; don't hedge points. If you are writing a product release, two pages of copy are maximum; if the story can be written in one page, don't stretch it. Provide application data, availability, specifications, and prices. If you have further interesting backup data, add a note to the editor that more information is available. This could lead to a longer article.

If a release is more than one page, type in "more" at the bottom of all pages except the last. At the end of the release type in "end," "30," "###," or some other such designation to show the editor that he has received all pages—even if the release is only one page. On multi-page releases take the time to staple all pages together (one staple, at upper left).

Set up a review and approval system for both draft and final releases. A simple system is to place a large stamp on each review copy with a space for the name of each individual who should review and approve each release. Opposite each name have spaces for the reviewer's initials and a date. Be certain each release is initialed and dated by each person. Don't bypass anyone, and don't accept the review copy back without the reviewer's initials and the date. Even though this seems like passing the buck, *protect yourself* by using some methodical review system.

Indicate both the date that the release is being issued and the date that the information may be used. In most cases they will be the same, but for the latter you may want to note "immediate," "morning newspapers of January 5," "not before September 11," or some similar indication. The limiting dates are particularly effective for press conferences where some media representatives require advance information in order to meet publication deadlines, but where you don't want the data to appear in print before the conference.

For a literature release, a paragraph is adequate. However, send along a copy of the literature; prove to the editor that it exists. Also, many magazines maintain a literature file of backup information for future articles. Your literature, if of any value, is likely to be placed in that file. Send a photograph of the cover only if a particular magazine is likely to use it; most don't.

Although personnel, organization, and financial releases are not used by all magazines or newspapers as editorial material, send them anyway. Editors rarely discard releases without first scanning them. This type of information can be interesting "background" to the editor whether or not he uses it actively. Merely by reading it he will know a little more about your company and possibly have greater interest when one of your "good" releases reaches him.

Give full name, title, address, and telephone number of the person to answer editorial or technical questions. Also note where to send customer inquiries. If no inquiries are desired except on company letterhead, state this clearly. Surprisingly, some releases omit even the company street or city address, or are very vague about the location of the particular division involved.

In any release—long or short—be specific. Don't make every other paragraph a capabilities blurb or an "executive quote." (Of course, cutting out the latter can be a step toward your forced relocation at a new company.) If it's politically necessary to include company or executive paragraphs, place these at the very end where the editor can easily delete them.

Don't repeat releases, and don't send out the same release a few months later written in a slightly different manner. Editors become wary of organizations that submit a "new product" release more than once. If your release didn't receive good acceptance the first time, maybe there was something wrong with it—or the product. Analyze the content and correct the errors for the next release.

Don't try to put something over on editors. Usually the editors will have good working knowledge of the technology involved in your release. If in doubt, they will ask questions. Of course, they can sometimes be fooled; but once burnt, they will probably rarely, if ever, use your company's, or agency's, releases. The taint is likely to remain on the names listed as PR or technical contacts also.

Editors, almost universally, will take a negative attitude to pressure. Don't try to tie an ad campaign to a release by telling the editor that your company's ad schedule in his magazine depends on whether or not he uses your release; chances are your release will automatically be dumped. Most editors try to keep editorial and advertising separated. An editor occasionally may decide to use a product release from a company because he feels a good reader response could lead to future increased ad revenue, but only if he also feels the product is of interest anyway to the magazine's readers. This is his editorial prerogative. Any attempt to pressure his choice of editorial content by promise or by threat is almost certain to have negative results.

This doesn't mean you should not follow up your releases occasionally by telephone calls to the editors. If not overdone, this can bring good results. When your release is particularly important, call key editors just after the time you estimate copies have reached them. Offer to provide added information to back up any points. Most editors will not take offense at this procedure—unless it is repeated too often—and may even accept your offer of more information.

For especially timely releases, such as annual reports, financial results, or corporate changes, deliver releases to all local newspaper editors personally or by messenger service. You may also find it worthwhile to use a wire service for rapid delivery to out-of-town newspapers and the financial press.

In addition to these general points, try to make the editor's job a little easier. The easier a release is to edit, the more likely that it will be used—and the more likely that the proper facts will be included. The editor has limited magazine space available; he will nearly always cut a release—sometimes drastically. He won't waste his efforts and magazine space on flowery or useless language. This might be the difference between his using or not using your release.

Some basic points are:

- Double space all typing
- Use pica type; elite may be acceptable, but avoid script or italic fonts
- Don't use all caps
- Be certain all lettering is clear and legible
- Leave at least 1-inch margins on all sides
- Use standard abbreviations
- Underline only really important or unusual information
- Print your releases on white paper in black ink, one side only; avoid mimeograph, spirit, diazo, or office copier methods

Photographs

Whenever possible, include a photograph with your release, However, despite the ancient and revered adage about a picture versus a thousand words, don't try to substitute a photograph for necessary written information. Provide all the necessary data. Then attach a photograph as an illustration and to prove that the equipment exists. For a circuit, attach a good line print that is compact enough to fit into the format of the article that might be printed.

Identify all prints on the back with company name and title of the equipment. A rubber stamp is very useful for the company identification and is not likely to damage the print. If you must write on the print, use a felt-tip pen. Also include a suggested caption for each illustration. This can be either on a sheet glued or taped *to the back* of each print or included as a paragraph at the bottom of the release. Be certain that the ink on the separate sheet is dry before attaching the sheet to the print so that the lettering won't transfer to the face of the print.

Send good, clean, high-contrast black and white prints. The most economical and practical size is 5 X 7. An 8 X 10 will be usable for most editors, but is more expensive and rarely shows more detail than a 5 X 7—and usually the editor will reduce the image even from the 5 X 7 format. A 4 X 5, although economical, sometimes causes problems for the editor— particularly if the print is not perfect. Normally, the editor will prefer to reduce the image rather than enlarge it. Remember, reduction hides defects; enlargement stresses them.

Use a professional, industrial photographer either from your own staff or from an outside service. Don't try to save money by having the picture taken by the marketing manager's assistant or a secretary who happens to own an Instamatic camera with a package of flash-cubes, or even a 35-mm camera with a miniature strobe. Don't have the corner drug store develop the film and make the prints.

Don't sacrifice print quality to save a few cents. Magazine editors are interested in the quality of their product as much as you are of yours. If a photo is poor and won't reproduce well, it probably won't even be considered for use.

Keep people out of equipment photos unless they serve a purpose. Especially keep out miniskirted secretaries or even professional models. These photos are fun to take—and most editors probably enjoy looking at a pretty girl. Take them if you want, but give the prints to your secretary to give to her boyfriend. Don't waste time and money sending them to the magazines.

Some technical magazines will use girlie shots but most will not or will relegate them to obscure locations. For instance, many magazines have "major," "feature," and "regular" product presentations, ranging in length from more than one page to a fraction of a page. It is likely that the product with a girlie photo would be considered only for the fraction spot, unless the editor thought enough of the product to request new photo-graphs, a procedure that might delay publication of a timely item. A safe procedure, if you must use girls or men in your photos *for political reasons*, is to keep them to one side so that the editor can crop them out without ruining the product view.

However, in many cases people in the photos are necessary to explain the equipment to advantage. For such occasions don't hesitate to include people, but make them actively a part of the scene. Have them do something that serves a purpose in the photo; be certain that in both appearance and costume they are realistic.

Carefully protect all prints when mailing. You can't take too many precautions in this matter. (Another advantage of smaller prints is that they are easier to protect than large ones.)

Sandwich prints between two pieces of heavy chipboard, cut a bit larger than the prints, and tape this sandwich to prevent the prints from falling out. Although not recommended, some PR personnel staple photographs to the release. In such cases, be absolutely certain the staple does not damage part of the photograph that is to be reproduced—and still use cardboard protection. Never use paper clips. These almost always damage the prints and necessitate cropping, sometimes of an important area.

Use realistic photos. Most editors quickly spot retouching on a print and immediately question its authenticity. A heavily retouched photo indicates not only to the editor but also to the reader of his magazine that possibly the piece of equipment doesn't really exist.

Don't send expensive color prints unless the editor requests them. Many magazines don't use color; others use color only in special "feature" spots. Note on your release if color prints are available. The editor will contact you if he wants them.

Know the Media

Many "how to" articles and handbooks on preparation of news releases stress writing to the level of the least informed reader. This fundamental idea has merit, but to follow it you will likely have to prepare several versions of each release. In all cases, know the proposed "reader" and use language he will understand. Even when long explanations are necessary, keep sentences short and to the point without "writing down" to the reader.

Certainly the average daily newspapers want releases that can easily be rewritten as news items for their nontechnical readers. For them, eliminate jargon, except for one or two "teaser" phrases, and minimize all but the most dramatic specifications. However, the exact opposite is necessary for the technical magazines. Their readers usually have scientific backgrounds and understand standard technical jargon. Don't write below their level. Eliminate "cute" phrases, provide adequate specifications, and stick to the facts stated in the language the readers use in their daily work.

For the financial press, once again, special releases are necessary if you are aiming directly at that medium. Send copies of *all* releases to financial editors for their background files, but prepare specific releases whenever only financial data are involved. Although all press releases should be reviewed and approved by both the relevant technical and administrative executives before they are sent, be especially certain that all financial releases are approved by the company financial officers and by the top executive management.

Preferably, releases should be mailed to editors by name and title. If you really can't take the time to determine the correct name, address your release to "editor," "product editor," "news editor," or other such title, which at least is better than using a wrong name. Releases addressed by name to an editor years after he left a particular magazine or newspaper are likely to receive wastebasket treatment. Editors do change jobs, just as you do, and you should keep up to date as a matter of etiquette and good PR, if nothing else.

Mailing list maintenance may seem expensive, but it is worthwhile. Up-to-date books are available which list editors of most publications. The masthead of each magazine or newspaper always contains names of the editors. If you update your mailing list every few months, you'll keep abreast of possible changes. Select a proper mailing list. To do this you must first know something about each periodical—its format, its content, its readers, its fields of interest. Don't spend time and money sending releases on spectroscopy to a computer magazine unless there is a computer involved, and don't send releases on computers to an electro-optical magazine unless optics are involved.

If you routinely submit releases over a range of several categories, code your mailing list adequately so that only the proper periodicals receive each release. There are several methods of doing this, depending on the addressing equipment you use. Know your system well enough to be able to use such a code.

You might even consider sending different versions of one basic release to various destinations, depending upon the interest of each periodical. Certainly a release sent to the financial press should be different from one sent to technical magazines. Any increase in cost will be overcome by the increase in acceptances.

Summary

To assure consistent acceptance of his news releases, the writer must know the interests of the particular editors and of the magazines' readers; must prepare valid, newsworthy releases; and must submit the releases in the proper, easy-to-use format that facilitates their use. He can't expect every release to be used every time, but if a release is prepared properly, if the information is important and timely, and if his mailing list is correct, a high percentage of acceptance is likely.

CHAPTER 9

An Analytical Approach to the Development of Technical Sales Literature

HARRY W. SMITH, JR.
President, Harry W. Smith, Inc.
Technical Information Programs
New York City

First, Be Crystal Clear About FUNCTION

Too many sales literature projects are carried through to completion without *clear and continuing agreement* (among sales chief, product chief, market chief, sales promotion chief, technical writer and designer of printing) as to the *function* each particular piece of literature is to perform.

Projects are frequently launched (and budgeted) for one purpose, but acquire additional and different purposes as they go along. Watch out for "too many cooks" and "tails that wag dogs."

The following grid may help categorize common functions of technical sales literature. It may widen the view of rut-followers; it may help you to keep kibitzers (especially of senior title) from diverting or embellishing or editing you into an impotent result. But it is introduced here to demonstrate how—in sales literature as in so many other creative fields—FORM FOLLOWS FUNCTION.

The column headings distinguish between "uses" or "types" of technical literature. The row labels distinguish between different "scopes" or "specializations."

Pause here and try to spot the *single* cell in which your current project fits. Don't expect one printed piece to fit more than one or two cells. It's a common error in doing literature to attempt "bibles" presumed (and *only* presumed) to be able to serve all functions.

Typical specifications, by column and row (see Table 1):

Special Campaign Literature should be brief, dramatic, and stick to one subject—the argument of the campaign. Evidence and detail presented should pertain only thereto. No room for extras while campaigning. The popular label "bulletin"—as in Bull. No. 307—is appropriate, for it implies the "news" and "now" of a special situation.

Campaign technical literature is not designed, necessarily, to stand alone. It's only one element of a total "attack" or "drive." Design it to set up a sales call, to work in the hands of a salesman, or to be the followup piece which goes with personal correspondence in the push to close business—depending upon how the sales campaign is planned. It's an instrument, but it must have power. You don't have to research and develop it to last forever (although many a good "bulletin" keeps popping up for years).

Such literature may be product-oriented if the campaign's on one product; recipient-oriented if the attack is on a special group (designers, researchers, corporate officers, appropriation committeemen, purchasing agents, or whomever); market-oriented; region-oriented; or circumstance-oriented—but its special orientation must show.

You'll know in a hurry when your work in this field is well conceived. Those who are running (and paying for) the campaign will let you know as their big push proceeds.

Buyer Reference Literature is more narrowly (and archaically) called "catalog" literature. It *does* have to stand alone. Often it's designed for the professional expert whom your salesman has trouble getting through to. It has to be so obviously helpful at the sleeves-rolled-up level that it shouts "save me; you'll need me."

The great and successful "consolidated catalog files" (like Sweet's Architectural shelf) have demonstrated the business-building power of our B-2 cell—literature which is conceived for library reference *when the specifier of goods is actively searching for answers* (not impatiently reading his mail)—literature which is *market-specialized* (as to specifying engineers and architects).

Such literature must be full of selection information and tables, plus application guidelines. Available sizes, capacities, and variations are vital. Somewhere must be given (usually on the back cover) all the names, addresses and phone numbers to use when the buyer comes to the point of action or inquiry.

Textbook or Handbook Literature is recipient-specialized (e.g., for metallurgists, plant engineers, formulating chemists, nurse anesthetists). It's done not so much to sell as *to teach* (your special technology, of course), *to become that source of know-how* the trade is most beholdin' to, to qualify you and your experts as the *top authority in the field*. And a good job in this category keeps working year after year after year.

Table 1.

Specialized	Type Special campaign literature	Buyer reference literature	Textbook ...handbook literature	"Doorbell" literature	"Reaction" literature	...other sales jobs
By Product						
By Market						
By Recipient						
By Other Focus						

I'm reminded of IR's famous compressed air handbook and SKF's hard cover masterpieces on roller bearing design. Less heroically, there's a 24-page spring designer's guide (complete with graphical design procedure) we did last year for Sandvik, or the little breast-pocket compilations of useful data which the alloy and specialty steelmakers spread throughout the metal industries.

When you develop such literature you are helping the *product* or *market* managers in your firm more than the *line* or *regional* sales managers.

Most industrial firms selling truly technical products *want* to author text, manual, and handbook literature for the technical prestige it insures and its long working life, BUT fewer will be easily appropriate for it after they measure the hundreds of expert-hours involved. Your job is to show that you know enough, or can learn enough fast enough, to control the experts and minimize their time.

"Doorbell" Literature is my favorite name for that which is periodical (or otherwise persistent)—in making *sales* calls on lists of known prospects more frequently than can the field sales force. Enter: data-sheet series, technical newsletters, external magazines, page-by-page handbooks or manuals, regular application reports, and single-sheet product presentations (at which, incidentally, German industry excels).

They can ring doorbells and gain entrance into offices, workrooms, and conferences not easy for the salesman to penetrate.

Important details: The field salesman should know it, use it, and consider it *his* personal message to *his* prospects. It can be engineered either for throwaway or for keep-and-file; in the former case it must make a clear memorable point, and in the latter it must contain something so valuable the recipient won't dare discard. In distributor selling, imprints (or at least space therefore) are indicated. The style and "personality" of the periodical is almost as important as the selection and helpfulness of its technical content. It should have a written editorial policy and raison d'etre. And mostly, stick to it—power is cumulative. As sales managers are well aware, a "yes" in business (as in old-fashioned love) is merely the 15th "no."

"Reaction" Literature is another of our own home-grown labels—this time for what the adman would probably refer to as direct mail. But we just can't call solid, helpful, technical information "advertising," although some of our clients do. In any event this is the breed of technical literature which issues a proposition, makes an offer, encloses a reply card, or challenges the disbeliever.

It's the form of technical literature that openly talks "you," Mr. Recipient. It must be brief. It never gives the whole story with selection guides, procedure and footnotes, else the reader will feel sated and left with nothing further to come to you to learn. Be exhaustive with your "textbook" and your "buyer reference" literature, if indicated—but not here. Yet, to win "reaction" from the cool and calculating technical experts who specify in our world, you have to be sound, clear and convincing—and know which are the problems currently bugging the prospects (and write to them).

So much for definitions and distinctions. Let us assume that you now know what you're up to and why—from the sales executive's standpoint—and have found the cell or cells of our grid in which you are working.

Next, Comes THE PACKAGE

Look at the "packaging" job from four standpoints before you lay into researching, interviewing, pigeon-holing, designing, and writing (which are the "craft" steps):

1) the *physical* packaging,
2) the *copy* packaging,
3) the *visual* packaging, and finally
4) the *budget* packaging.

THE *PHYSICAL* PACKAGE

Specifications for the physical (or shall we say the printer's) package—size, pagination, paper, fold, cover, binding, and envelope— are fixed primarily by the manner in which the literature will be used in the field. Specifications for content—length, format, copy, and visualization—are fixed primarily by the sales job you undertake to do. First, the former. Let's consider size.

The standard 8-1/2" × 11" size is strongly favored by almost everyone today. If the distribution list is large and the pages few, 8-1/2 × 11 folds twice to letter-envelope size or once to 6 × 9 envelope size, and can become a self-mailer to save significant postage; if your handiwork must make it onto shelves of engineering offices, 8-1/2 × 11 can be bound with or without printed backbone a dozen ways and whole series of specialized bulletins assembled in remarkably varied choices of ideal binders; if your sales literature's destination is (via desk top) to drawer or filing cabinet, 8-1/2 × 11 is almost mandatory; if hard working shophands will thumb through your works again and again, varnished or laminated covers make 8-1/2 × 11 practical; and the size is decreed for AIA-coded engineer/builder/architect buying literature, and many consolidated files.

Odd sizes are occasionally justified: these steel-company shop-handy breast-pocket-size useful-data items; ICI-America's justly famous self-mailing *Chemmuniqué* of inside-coat-pocket dimensions; and impressive textbook-size or handbook-size "manuals" in classical hard or semi-hard permanent bookbinding. Even these last-named are increasingly going to 8-1/2 × 11 (as are so many college texts in paperback), what is called "perfect" binding, and offset printing from typed master sheets.

Once in a while the outsize piece is requested for "executive prestige," although I prefer simply binding 8-1/2 × 11 on the short side for equal effect.

There are thousands of such "craft" or "printer's" or "physical" details to settle. I treat just one here to make the points that: a) choice is not arbitrary, but dictated by function (and dollar practicality in this day of outlandish production and mailing costs), and b) the physical package should be well thought out and "dummied up" *before* you undertake the *copy* and *visual* parcels of your technical-journalism-for-sales.

THE COPY PACKAGE

Here we are, now, in the technical writer's home court—*copy*—where men and women need least orientation. Still, there are determinants in developing technical sales literature which should be noted, if not treated in detail.

Recall the grid of literature functions on Table 1. Working in a different cell (to a different sales function) may well mean working in an entirely different . . .

- *STYLE*
- *TECHNICAL DEPTH*
- *SIZE OF BITE*
- *TYPE (AND DEGREE) OF DOCUMENTATION*
- *OUTLINE (OR ARGUMENT)*

Examples: campaigning style is more attacking than is reference style; textbook literature can go to greater *technical depth* than other forms; the *bite size* of persistent doorbell literature should be small since you'll soon return with another bite; *documentation* may be reduced to references if your company's authority in the field is accepted (as in handbook literature), but elaborated to a variety of convincing "examples" or "proofs" to maximize response to reaction-type literature; the *outline* for descriptive literature may run from cause to effect, but in campaign literature *net effect* (ultimate customer benefit) is invariably the lead-off, the headline, the stopper, the opener.

But there's another, and more important, aspect of flexibility in style, depth, bite-size, documentation, and outline; that is matching the *reader* as well as the sales function.

All readers are *not* alike—in interest, scope, behavior, or understanding—especially in the technical world. Glowing proofs of this are the pole-to-pole differences among the 3,000 trade, technical, and business publications in this country—no two alike, and each is exactly right for its special readership (otherwise it wouldn't survive in the hard worlds of editorial loyalty and advertising support).

For the Swedish Export Association some years back I prepared a piece on the "101 Different American Industrial Languages," in which the very grammars and glossaries of different trades, industries, job titles, and levels of reader erudition were shown to constitute almost mutually unintelligible tongues. Nor was Oxford English or "basic" English the Swedish exporter's answer, where cordial welcome in the States through sales literature was concerned.

But, "jargon" apart (assuming that you here are all properly schooled in the tongue which earns your daily bread), think about matching your *style, depth, size-of-bite, documentation,* and *outline* in sales literature to these differing characteristics of different reader groups. . . .

INDUSTRIAL OR PROFESSIONAL SPHERE
DEGREE OF TECHNICAL SAVVY
PATIENCE WITH PRINTED MATERIAL
SUBJECTS OF ENTHUSIASTIC CONCERN
LIKELY ACTION IF IMPELLED THERETO
INFLUENCE ON BUYING DECISION

For example: Consider the language of the metal industries versus that of the medical profession; consider the patience of the chemical engineer with formulas and flow diagrams versus that of his budget committee; consider the relative enthusiasms of purchasing agent and chief engineer for price information, or for service life data; consider the chain of action a research man must follow when he needs a piece of equipment; consider the classic relationship in buying decision of the thoughts of product designer, production chief, and purchasing agent. These are *reader* determinants of your work.

There's no doubt that you'll arrive at proper matches of technique both to sales function and to reader idiosyncrasy—*if* you worry about them more than you savor your *own* copy tastes, or try to adapt to your bosses'.

Now, to make the transition from determinants of the *copy* package to determinants of the *visual* package, let me elaborate on a phrase I've been teasing you with—"size-of-bite."

Good sales literature proceeds a bite at a time—be the whole piece of literature a snack or a meal or a banquet. One might define the "bite" as the "scope"—in idea or amount of information—which is tastiest and most quickly digestible by the reader.

Whatever the appropriate bite-size may be in copy or data, it has interesting limits in visual exposition. *Maximum* visual bite-size is what admen call a "visual spread"—two facing pages seen as a unit at once. Every turn of a page is, so to speak, a new visual bite. Therefore, in your sales literature (with the possible exception of the textbook type in which you rely upon student-persistence by reader) try to restrict your largest bite to two facing pages.

On the small end—for little bites—use the principle of "insulation" to package them. To a designer of sales literature, "insulation" may be provided by a separate color area overprinted with a bite, a box, a column cut off from the remainder of the spread by background or rule, special use of white space, a section in different type face or color, or an appliqué or odd shape on the spread. The goal of "insulation" is to prevent the cross-circuiting of ideas—to keep the meat out of the mouth until the potatoes are swallowed. One could say, to "separate" or "set off" or "dissociate" or "sequence" your bites—to prevent visual "stuffing."

THE VISUAL PACKAGE (TECHNIGRAPHICS)

What are the visual elements of *technical* exposition?

They include: charts, and diagrams, and photomicrographs, and mathematical formulas, and plots, and engineering drawings, and nomographs, and tabular arrangements of data, and cutaways, and instrument pen traces, and sequence sketches, and flow sheets, and symbols, and enumerations (lists), and actual attached samples (swatches and paint chips), and assembly explosions, and sample calculations, and, and, and—all in addition to the photograph in its infinite variety and use.

And what do we use such elements for in doing technical literature? Here's a list (a form of visual in itself) which may widen your view. We use visuals in technical exposition for. . . .

Abbreviation	*Quantification*	*Orientation*
Acceleration	*Organization*	*Reference*
Emphasis	*Computation*	*Certification*
Association	*Documentation*	*Internationalization*
Dissociation	*Data Storage*	*Selection*
Explanation	*Demonstration*	*Summary*

Let's run through them again—with just one elaborating thought each: abbreviation (8 feature spotted in one drawing); acceleration (instant communication); emphasis (the close-up photo); association (the several variables in a mathematical evaluation of an effect); dissociation (keeping the example, in illustration, from interrupting the argument, in words); explanation (any diagram); quantification (any coordinate plot of a function); organization (flowcharts); computation (the nomogram or formula); documentation (test data); demonstration (an "example" calculation); data storage (for which the tabular arrangement was invented); orientation (the cutaway drawing or explosion showing part in relation to whole); reference (parametric families of plotted data, or corrosion tables); certification (ASTM or other ratings); internationalization (no need to translate the pictorial, diagrammatic or internationally symbolized); selection (the size vs. capacity tables in all catalogs); summary (enumerated lists).

Such functions for visual elements in technical sales literature are far more than "accessory" or "incidental." Consider the visual element in exposition as a "wordless paragraph"—a bite in the meal you serve—a critical element in the flow of your argument.

To talk about how to handle the visual element would be craft, and well beyond our time limitation—there being as much to it as to composition by sentence and paragraph. But we have a visual definition of TECHNI-GRAPHICS which may guard you from wandering and from an oversight (see Figure 1). It shows that *four disciplines* must intersect to do it right—to produce techni-graphics which work and which are respected by very precise and opinionated technical readers. And, now, money. . . .

THE BUDGET PACKAGE

Surely, the first point to get across to the sales executive who needs the technical literature you must produce is that what he (at first blush) considers to be the cost (travel, photography, art, type, paper, printing, binding, envelopes, postage, et al.) is only half, *or less*, of the full cost.

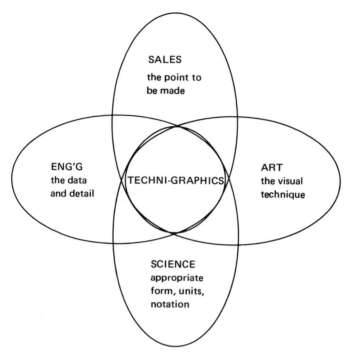

Figure 1.

Your time and overhead and the time of the talent you engage (to say nothing of the time of the authorities from whom the two of you must draw information) will more than match the "bills and expense accounts." Actual cost ratios for recent sales literature projects in our shop were: 3-to-2, 3-to-1 and 11-to-9—the higher fraction always being the fee for time and talent only.

Second budget guide: Compute the total cost of sales literature in terms of "cost per call." Consider the delivery of a copy to a worthwhile recipient-reader as an actual sales visit. Our clients do, and come up with numbers roughly between 50¢ and $2.50 per "call." Sales managers who spend $25 to $50 for each personal sales call won't flinch.

PART FOUR

Evaluating
Technical
Communication

Grading Technical Reports with the Cassette Tape Recorder: The Results of a Test Program at the United States Air Force Academy*

LT. COL. DAVID L. CARSON
Director of Technical Writing
United States Air Force Academy

CAPT. JOHN B. MC TASNEY
USAF

The Need for Better Grading Methods

Instructors have perennially complained about the onerous demands of grading. One of the reasons for this general dissatis-

* The authors are indebted to Professor John S. Harris of Brigham Young University who formulated and developed many of the basic concepts and to those members of the Academy's English faculty whose hard work made the test program possible.

faction lies not in the average instructor's reluctance to devote his time to improving his student's skills in a particular field, but in his inability, given the limitations of conventional grading systems, to impart sufficient knowledge to the student within the time parameters available. If a physics instructor took the time to write out a detailed explanation of a student's errors on an examination, for example, he could spend almost as much time as the student took to take the test. Current instructor/student ratios deny such luxuries and future prospects look no brighter. The problem becomes even more acute for the English teacher in the advanced composition or technical writing course. If he wishes to develop his students' writing ability to the utmost, he will have them write frequently, he will grade each piece of writing thoroughly, and he will make as many comments as his time permits to help the student become a better writer. This means he may have to grade as many as fifteen writing assignments of various lengths in a semester. The barrier to learning which he must face every time he sits down before a pile of themes is efficiency in communications. If he is grading an average five-hundred word theme written by an average college student, his workload will seldom permit him to spend more than fifteen minutes grading it. Moreover, if he were to adequately assess that theme in his own handwritten script, he could very easily end up writing a seven-hundred word analysis of that five-hundred word paper. This would, of course, take far more time than is reasonable to expect, no matter how dedicated the instructor.

DISADVANTAGES OF CONVENTIONAL WRITTEN COMMENTS

Faced with these pressures—the desire to impart the benefit of his expertise and the restrictions of time—the instructor has been forced to compromise. Instead of a lengthy written analysis of a piece of writing, the instructor falls back on his own system of coded markings—hence the symbols *K*, *ww*, *repet*, *ss*, *//*, and so forth which we have all found written in red on our own papers.

The problem is that these marks are very meaningful to the man who understands the complex jargon of syntax, but they mean almost nothing to the neophyte who is unfamiliar with that code. As a result, subsequent writing for most such students is just one more stab into the unknown world of conventional rhetorical practice. If the teacher had time to explain why the sentence was not parallel (*//*), or how to avoid the fused sentence (*FS*), the student might be expected to learn something. But the cryptic marks which refer him to the equally cryptic explanations in his dictionary or his grammar book only tend to confuse him more. Let us consider that five-hundred word theme again.

A POSSIBLE SOLUTION

If instructors could take the time to explain why the sentence in question was not parallel, without exceeding the limits of their allotted time, they would be delighted, and the student might eventually learn to write sentences which were syntactically balanced. Cassette grading seemed to offer the possibility of attaining these goals, at least in part; it was with this hope that we undertook a pilot cassette grading program in the technical writing course at the United States Air Force Academy. The cassette system offered this opportunity because cassette recorders are economically priced and are readily available. Cassette tapes are also cheap, and they offer a greater compactness and more foolproof method of recording than any other recording device available. The average cassette recorder weighs a mere three pounds and is thus highly portable. Nearly all such recorders can be powered by either flashlight batteries or alternating current, and most are built to hold all of the required accessories internally. Moreover, the cassette tape is a self-contained unit which fits easily into a shirt pocket.

Other advantages which suggested its use were the suspected ready availability of student-owned playback equipment, and the advantages of privacy gained by use of the portable earphone.

Course Description

English 430, Technical Writing, is a required course for all science and engineering majors. It is offered in the fall and is open to seniors and selected juniors. The first twelve of thirty-nine lessons consist of an in-class workshop throughout which the instructor reviews such matters as grammar, punctuation, organization, non-verbal aids, and format. The students write short (five-hundred word) themes, mechanism descriptions, process descriptions, and any other short exercises the instructor deems necessary. He traditionally has graded all writing assignments conventionally.

REQUIRED REPORTS

Halfway through the course, the student writes a 1000-1500 word Minor Report on a technical subject of his choice using the technical indexes, abstracts, and other technical sources available in the Academy library. To complete the course, he also writes a Major Report of 3000-4500 words. This report usually requires in-depth research and often involves original experimentation within the area of the student's major field. In the fall of 1971, the course enrollment numbered 367 students.

INSTRUCTORS

Of the eight instructors assigned to teach the course, several also taught other courses, and all had at least four semesters of experience in teaching composition. Their initial response to the concept of cassette grading ranged from keen interest to rather strong opposition. Only two instructors were very enthusiastic about the idea. The others understandably wished to withhold judgment until they had worked with the program. Several commented that gadgetry could never replace instructor competency and the personal touch in the teaching of writing.

QUESTIONNAIRE NUMBER 1

To determine student response before the program started, each student was asked to fill out a questionnaire as follows. At this time no course work had been cassette graded. Question 3 was included to assist us in determining how many playback units were needed for the students' use.

> This semester the Department of English will use cassette tape recorders experimentally to determine their effectiveness as a means of critiquing cadet writing. This method should allow the instructor to say more about a paper in less time using a fresh new medium. Since student improvement is the ultimate measure of any program's effectiveness, we will ask for your opinions at various times during the program. Please answer the following questions and add any comments you would like to make.
>
> 1. Do you consider the English instructor's conventional written comments on your paper to be a very effective way of improving your writing?
>
> Yes: 51%; No: 49%
>
> 2. Have you ever been critiqued by any other method? If Yes, please describe method, and was it a better system?
>
> Yes: 25%; No: 75%

3. Do you have access to a cassette tape recorder, either your own or someone else's, in the dormitory?

Yes: 93%; No: 7%

4. Would you like to participate in the cassette critiquing program?

Yes: 79%; No: 21%

5. Even though you may not have experienced cassette grading and critiquing, does it sound like a good idea to you?

Yes: 83%; No: 17%

Questionnaire results reflected enthusiastic student response as evidenced in questions 4 and 5, and their response to question 3 showed that 93% of them had access to cassette recorders in their dormitories.

Pilot Program

Prior to the semester's start, we ordered twelve Roberts Model 80 cassette recorders and 367 one-hour cassette tapes (one for each student) at a total cost of $1,029.80. Each participating instructor checked out one of these recorders and tape cassettes sufficient for his students. One instructor elected to use his own recorder; this left five recorders for student use.

RECORDERS FOR STUDENT USE

These recorders were placed for convenience behind the Media Services checkout counter at the Academy's Audio Visual Aids Center. Students were encouraged to use these recorders in the listening room provided nearby. They could log them out any time between 7:30 AM and 4:30 PM.

SUGGESTED INSTRUCTOR TECHNIQUE

Before beginning to grade, using the cassette system, the participating instructors were briefed on several suggested techniques. The seemingly best techniques derived from an unpublished paper generously provided by John S. Harris, Professor of English, Brigham Young University. It was suggested that instructors use his system as a point of departure. Harris' method consists of reading

THE HUMAN RESPIRATORY SYSTEM

INTRODUCTION

Plan of Development From an explanation of what the respiratory system **3***
is, this report describes its structure and function in detail. Besides the
learning value behind this information, it may excite one into repairing **4**
his respiratory system and keeping it fit for long life. The two most common diseases, emphysema and pneumonia, are described and illustrated. *omiT##*
philosophy

Definition of the Respiratory System The respiratory system *consists of* equals the
lungs and the passages leading toward them. The lungs are connected to
the exterior *atmosphere* by this series of passages: the nose, nasopharynx, larynx,
trachea and bronchi. These are relatively rigid structures which comprise the conducting portion of the respiratory system. The reason for
their rigidity is that they must stay open so air flows in when the
thoracic cavity is expanded. (2:337) Within the lungs the tubule system
further subdivides from the bronchi into bronchioles, respiratory
bronchioles, alveolar ducts and sacs, and alveoli. Figure 1 illustrates
these divisions and the functional units of the lung, the lobule, wherein **6**
are found the respiratory bronchiole, alveolar duct and sac, and alveoli.

Function of the Respiratory System The main *functions* function of the respiratory **7**
system is to provide for an **1** intake of oxygen by the blood and to **2** eliminate
carbon dioxide. These gaseous exchanges occur in respiratory tissu*e* in
the lungs. Functions of the conduction*g* division are to strain out particu-
late matter, wash and humidify air by fluid secretions of sereous and
mucous glands, and either warm or cool *incoming* air depending on the **8**
ambient temperature. (2:337) The lungs also function as an excretory
organ because water is lost in expired air. (2:360)

Figure 1. Sample student paper.

the paper and making comments simultaneously. To orient the student to the location of the taped comment with reference to his paper, and to minimize time consuming writing, Harris suggests that the instructor mark consecutive Arabic numerals in the right margin opposite the point in question. (See Figure 1.) However, instructors were given the freedom to use whatever methods they chose, but they were requested to minimize verbiage and to avoid unnecessary handwritten comments.

PROGRAM IMPLEMENTATION

All instructors cassette graded the Minor Report at the midpoint of the course. Individual techniques in actual practice varied as instructors attempted to develop a system best suited to themselves, and nearly everyone experienced the predictable difficulties encountered in working with a new medium. Some instructors, suddenly having the opportunity to explain as much as they wished, talked for an hour and a half about one single paper. Others experienced microphone fright and still others felt the need to erase and re-record whenever their diction was less than faultless. Some instructors continued to do a considerable amount of writing on their students' papers, and others could not critique the papers on tape while they read them for the first time. Instead, they read the paper through, making marginal notes, and then critiqued it on the tape.

After four days of grading, all instructors met to discuss their problems and to listen to several actual taped critiques which had been made in only twenty minutes. Later nearly all were, with practice, able to reduce their grading times considerably by eliminating unnecessary comments and by commenting as they read through the paper the first time.

MINOR REPORT RESULTS

The twenty-minute time is comparable to the time required to conventionally grade the same papers, in depth, and most instructors were able to achieve this level of competency. The cassette system, as a result, did not save instructor time, but it did enable

---

Footnotes to Figure 1.

    * Arabic numerals indicate points at which the instructor made tape recorded comments about this sample paper.

    ** All handwritten comments were made by the student during playback to clarify the instructors comments for future reference.

the instructor to convey to the student approximately three or four times as much information in a much more personally coherent manner.

When instructors returned the graded papers and cassette tapes to their students, they told them to page through the papers while listening to the tapes. They also encouraged the student to make handwritten clarifications of the instructor's comments right on the paper for future reference. (See Figure 1.) To permit the student to ask questions, however, instructors scheduled individual counseling sessions with each student.

STUDENT RESPONSE

During these conferences, 93% of all students gave a positive reaction to cassette grading, and very few asked for further clarification of instructor comments, whereas with conventional grading methods the instructor would have taken an average time of more than ten minutes to explain his written comments. As a result, most students used the counseling session to ask questions about what would be expected of them in the upcoming Major Report.

QUESTIONNAIRE NUMBER 2

To verify this rather surprising student response, we administered another Cassette Grading Questionnaire (as follows) to give students the opportunity to answer without coercive pressures in the anonymity of the classroom. The results of this questionnaire showed an even greater enthusiasm. Student handwritten comments indicated some of the reasons for their continued enthusiasm. Without being told what the system was supposed to do, most students perceived that the cassette method had achieved the goals we had hoped for. Interestingly, despite differences in instructor techniques, the results from Questionnaire 2 did not vary significantly among instructors.

MAJOR REPORT RESULTS

Instructors also cassette critiqued the 3000-word Major Reports and significantly reported an average grading time of forty minutes. This phenomenon was largely attributable to two factors working together. First, all instructors had become more proficient with the cassette method. Second, student writing was, in general, so improved that extensive comments were seldom necessary.

STUDENT RESPONSE

In short, scheduled conferences, students indicated the same high level of enthusiasm as they had done previously. And in another anonymous, end of course questionnaire, they again expressed the same degree of affirmation.

> The information you provided in our first questionnaire enabled us to improve our pilot program immensely. Since 93% said you had recorders available in the squadron and 83% wanted to participate, we pulled four recorders from the DFIT listening area, gave recorders to all the English 430 instructors, and cassette graded everyone in the course. By better use of our equipment in this way, the cost per student of this test program dropped considerably. With the same equipment in next year's course, we can cut the cost per student in half again.
>
> Now we need your reactions to being cassette graded in order to improve the program even more and to determine if it has been effective. Please answer the following questions and comment as you see fit.

1. Did you listen to the cassette critique of your Minor Report?

Yes: 98%; No: 2%

2. Did you have difficulty obtaining a recorder?

Yes: 2%; No: 98%

3. Was your instructor's taped critique meaningful?

Yes: 94%; No: 6%

4. Did his comments help you understand your mistakes?

Yes: 97%; No: 3%

5. Do you think cassette grading, overall, is better or worse than conventional grading methods?

Better: 94%; Worse: 6%

6. Do you think that cassette grading would have helped you in Freshman English?

Yes: 44%; No: 56%

7. Please make comments or suggestions concerning cassette grading.

OVERALL CRITICISMS

One of the more frequent initial objections from both students and instructors alike was directed toward the suspected high cost of the program, but the cost analysis below suggests their fears were unjustified. Other early instructor complaints centered upon the use of machines to replace face-to-face, interpersonal relationships. But again, by the program's end, most instructor apprehensions had been resolved by actual experience. In fact, the instructor who was the strongest objector reversed his position by the program's end.

The only instructor criticism which remained fairly constant throughout the program centered on time expended, but this was true partially because some instructors still experienced difficulty in adapting to the medium. One widespread criticism noted that grading in the instructor's office cubicles was extremely difficult because of the extraneous noise picked up by the microphone through the only partially enclosed partitions. Instructors were able to minimize this disadvantage, however, by controlling recording levels manually and by working close to the microphone.

Cost Analysis

Although the following statistics indicate the relatively high cost of $2.80 per student, it should be remembered that this is pilot program cost. By the use of the same machines and tapes in subsequent years, the cost would be reduced considerably.

12 Roberts Model 80 Recorders @ $50.34	$ 604.08
367 Scotch C60 cassettes @ $1.16	425.72
	$1029.80

$1029.80/367 students = *$2.80 per student*

Assuming a four-year recorder and tape life and an unoptimistic straight line depreciation in value to $100 for all twelve recorders, the average cost for recorders over the four-year period becomes $504. Further assuming that the tapes will depreciate to a negligible value in that same period, their average value for four years is $212.86. An estimated 1600 students would use this equipment, producing a projected cost per student of $\frac{(\$504 + \$212)}{1600} = \$00.45$. Obviously, since adequate equipment may be purchased even more cheaply than this cost basis indicates, cost is not a major consideration so long as the system produces desired results.

Findings

The first and most obvious finding revealed in the experiment is that the students' enthusiasm for cassette grading never waned. Some of this fervor was undoubtedly generated by their fondness for innovation. Frankly, this, if true, would help justify continuation of the program; interest in the critique of a paper is unusual enough to warrant inclusion on the credit side of the ledger. And, strangely enough, student interest in the program increased after the Minor Reports were graded by unusually severe standards. Initially, only 79% of the students thought they would like to participate in a cassette grading program. (See Questionnaire Number 1.) After they had listened to instructor critiques of their Minor Reports, 94% stated that they thought cassette grading better than conventional grading. (See Questionnaire Number 2.)

Student comments revealed some bases for the continuing enthusiasm:

1. Instructor explanations were more complete and more completely intelligible.
2. The tapes revealed the grader's initial reaction to the report and linked his comments to a general train of developing thought.
3. The cassette critique was easier to understand than the normally cryptic marks.
4. The cassette technique was more personal.
5. The student could read the passage in question while the instructor commented on it.

Instructor explanations were usually more complete because the instructor could provide more intelligible information by voice in the time allotted. Moreover, he was not limited by space on the page. In seconds he could read the passage involved, cite the applicable grammatical rule, use the original passage as an example, and then suggest several ways to correct the error. Going beyond simple mechanics, where knowledge of general grammatical rules provided some common student-instructor background for communication, the more difficult and particular problems of organization, style, and syntax (which were almost impossible to handle adequately with written comments) could be explained quickly on a cassette tape.

The system permits the instructor to verbalize his reaction to the student's words and their arrangement. He can refer to earlier passages; he can outline the student's paper, and then suggest several alternative organizational structures that might have been more effective. Again he can use the student's passages and paragraphs for examples to provide a verbal cut-and-paste editing job. Written critiques of equal depth, using conventional abbreviations, would require several pages and at least twice as much instructor time.

As we suggested earlier, an instructor's written comments provide only dim insights into his meanings. Frequently, an instructor refrains from commenting on a specific point for fear a later clarification in the paper will negate his comment. Often the student never clarifies, and the instructor, distracted by subsequent errors, forgets the earlier question. Using the cassette, he does not hesitate to comment, because he is reacting as a reader would. If he errs, he may easily rectify his error later by whatever explanation is necessary, or he may easily erase any inappropriate comments.

A major reason why written critiques fail is that the student must often reread the pertinent passage several times before he understands it sufficiently in context to relate it to the cryptic written commentary of the professional proofreader. Most instructor explanations are more successful on tape because they are presented in an uncomplicated, conversational diction which tends to simplify discussion of formal points of style, syntax, and grammar. In addition, the instructor may, if he wishes, suggest several possible revisions to help him make his point.

Giving the lie to some preliminary concern over the impersonal, mechanistic nature of the cassette system, significant numbers of students volunteered the information that they thought the tape was more personal. In fact, one student stated during a conference that the immediacy of the tape so overwhelmed him that he had to turn it off. Several others humorously commented on the efficacy of their instructor's ironic tone, but most suggested that human speech with its coherent patterns and its variations in volume, tone, inflection, and pace helped greatly to increase the student's comprehension of his instructor's meaning.

In conventional grading systems, penmanship becomes an important part of the system, and, although instructors never consciously write cryptically, their comments are often unintelligible to students, so much so that the student begins to dislike the critique. Moreover, masses of red scribbling on a page create a rather unpleasant visual reinforcement of an unpleasant situation. The frequency of student comments on Question 1 of the first questionnaire points out their concern with this aspect of conventional grading, and they seemed quite pleased that cassette grading eliminated it. They also frequently seemed to like the fact that their grade need not appear anywhere on the paper for others to see.

Auditory reinforcement of visual perception is difficult to measure, but the tape provides obvious advantages by enabling the student to read his original passage as he simultaneously listens to the instructor's comments. Several students indicated on the second survey that they felt this method much more effective. Two admitted they usually ignored critiques, but nevertheless liked this method.

Recommendations

Modest pilot programs may be set up cheaply. With increasing interest in cassette recorders, a quick survey will probably show a considerable availability of both recorders and cassettes. This means that expenditures for student playback equipment may be kept at a minimum. If machines are necessary, prices for cassette recorders range from $18/unit for listen-only equipment to less than $29/unit for a record-and-listen machine for the instructor. Fifteen and thirty minute cassettes cost as little as 50¢ each at wholesale rates.* As a matter of interest, several students even indicated a willingness to buy their own tape cassettes for use in the program, and cassettes could easily be included on book or equipment lists as required student purchases. Moreover, our log book showed that student use of the listening equipment provided them was such that the program's cost per student could have been reduced $200 by buying four fewer machines.

Although cassette recorders are too new to have established maintenance records, Academy technicians advise, in general, that extra cost buys extras rather than reliability. We suggest consideration of several important features before purchasing equipment. For utility the recorder should have an ON-OFF switch on the microphone. This remote switch is not only more convenient to use, it also enables the instructor to make a smoother recording. The recorder should, furthermore, have a lock capability for the

* The $2.80 and 45¢ cost-per-student figures were based on $50 recorders and $1.16 cassettes.

rewind position. "T" handle controlled recorders with this feature are less expensive and are equally efficient as push-button types.

Cassette critiquing could obviously have application in other disciplines also. It provides the advantages of being able to

1. give more complete, detailed explanations in less time,
2. let the student listen as he looks at the mistakes, and
3. use inflection and volume in conveying exact instructor meanings which could carry over to critiques using any symbology.

Obviously, social science, philosophy, and history papers could be critiqued advantageously in this way. Because of the special non-verbal demands of basic and engineering sciences, cassette critiques might not prove as useful, but combined with short written derivations and solution steps the cassette critique could still have applications in these disciplines. As a matter of interest, several instructors from the scientific disciplines at the Academy have indicated an interest in cassette applications for their courses. More important, however, cassette critiquing could offer vast advantages throughout industry and education wherever management practices or learning situations lend themselves to the technique.

CHAPTER 11

External Examiners for Technical Writing Courses

DR. THOMAS M. SAWYER
College of Engineering
University of Michigan

Introduction

In the Fall 1973 issue of this journal "Examining Scientific Literature" was published. In that article I explained that, after visiting the University of Wales Institute of Science and Technology, I had experimented with the use of external examiners in my course in Scientific and Technical Communication and had persuaded professors emeriti of both engineering and English to come listen to my students' final oral presentations and to recommend a grade for each student. I have now been using this system for seven terms and have gradually modified the procedure and should like to describe how this system has evolved.

When I began this in the summer term of 1972 on my return from Wales, the Humanities Department offered relatively few sections of Scientific and Technical Communication. We had modified our curriculum in 1968 and substituted for the traditional freshman composition courses two terms of Great Books on the grounds that freshmen had little to write about but were woefully ignorant of the history and literature that educated persons, engineers included, should be familiar with. In place of freshman composition we had established a requirement that all *seniors* should be required to take at least one course in writing and speaking, on the grounds that *now* the students *did* have something to write about and welcomed, rather than resisted, help in learning how to write and speak. We offered them two options in this senior year: Scientific and Technical Communication in which the subject matter would be drawn from their engineering specialties, and Seminar in Writing and Speaking in which the subject matter would be drawn from other areas, often controversial public issues. Naturally there was a pipeline effect. It took three years before the freshmen who began with Great Books arrived in any significant numbers in these senior-level "rhetoric" courses.

Procedures

The surge began in the fall of 1972 and to handle the numbers of students enrolled in Scientific and Technical Communication with a limited staff, we experimented with a lecture-recitation format in which Professor W. E. Britton lectured on writing, I coached the students in public speaking, and teaching fellows handled the recitation sections. Dr. Wilmer Schnure, now at Bell Labs, was one of those teaching fellows and has described his experiences in his article, "An Engineer Teaches English" in the Fall 1974 issue of this journal.

By the winter term we had so many students that even the lecture-recitation format couldn't handle them all, so I was assigned a separate recitation section of my own while I continued to coach public speaking for the lecture sections. This individual section gave me an opportunity to repeat my experiment with external examiners in much the same way as I had begun. This time Professors Emeriti A. D. Moore of Electrical Engineering and Clark Hopkins of Classical Studies evaluated the students' lectures for me, and in the spring half-term Professors Clay Porter of Mechanical Engineering and Joseph Mullen of English did the same.

Up to this point I had been reluctant to suggest that these external examiners *read* the students' reports. I merely asked them to *listen* to the students' final ten-minute lectures. After all, they were donating their time, usually three separate class hours, without any remuneration at all.

During the fall term of 1973 we repeated the lecture-recitation format for the last time, and in the winter term I had two sections of my own. This time, with considerable trepidation, I collected the students' reports and offered them to the examiners—Warner Rice of English, Rudy Schmerl of Education, Arlen Hellwarth of

Electrical Engineering, and Harm Buning of Aerospace Engineering—
after the lectures, in case they would like to see the students'
writing as well. To my surprise they were all willing to take away
the reports, read them, write a paragraph or so of comment on
them, and recommend a grade.

By this time I had decided that the bigger the audience I could
get for these student lectures, the better. So early in the term I
asked each student to write a letter to the counselor in his department explaining that he was going to be put on public display and
asking for the counselor's approval of, or advice about, the topic
he would write and speak about. I distributed these letters to the
counselors with an explanatory note, and just before the final
lectures I distributed an invitation to them, and to the department
chairmen, with the dates, places, and schedules of these lectures.
The response was pretty good. Several of the counselors came to
hear how their students were doing, and now I am accustomed to
having several of them appear each term.

By the fall of 1974 I became even bolder. Thus far I had relied
on faculty from the University of Michigan to serve as external
examiners for me. Perhaps it was time to branch out and invite
people from other institutions and from industry. Our college
placement officer suggested some engineers from local industry and
I was pleased to find that they were very much interested in this
procedure and each of them accepted my invitation to serve as an
external examiner. Since Eastern Michigan University is only ten
miles away, I prevailed upon my friends, Milton Foster, chairman
of the English Department there, and Hoover Jordan, former
chairman, to come also. However, I couldn't resist inviting Robbins
Burling from Michigan's Anthropology Department after reading
his amusing article, "An Anthropologist Among English Teachers,"
in the October 1974 issue of *College Composition and
Communication.*

I needed six examiners because this time I had three sections of
the course, a total of thirty-six students, and I decided that it
would be more convenient for everyone to schedule the lectures
for three consecutive evening sessions, each three hours long, with
twelve students each evening, each student giving a ten-minute
lecture followed by a five-minute question period.

Moreover, by now I was persuaded that I *could* ask the
examiners to read the students' reports, but naturally, I couldn't
ask them to read all thirty-six. Twelve reports, however, didn't
sound like too much of a burden. This time I collected two copies
of each student's report on Friday afternoon, packaged them up,

and drove around town delivering them to the examiners so that they would have the weekend to look them over before the lecture sessions started on Monday evening.

I also tried to arrange the schedules so that each pair of examiners read and heard a variety of engineering topics. I felt that it would be pretty tiresome to evaluate nothing but civil engineers or electrical engineers. A sample evening's program is appended to this article.

Finally, it occurred to me, why not video-tape these lectures and present them on Ann Arbor Cable TV's Educational Channel? Fortunately, the Mechanical Engineering Department could let me borrow a TV camera and video-cassette recorder and the College of Engineering was willing to buy twelve hour-long video-cassettes for me to use and was even willing to pay for the time of a student technician to run the TV equipment for me.

Conclusions

The whole procedure worked very well, I thought. The examiners read the reports, heard the lectures, commented on both, and recommended a final grade. The students stopped in during the following days to see themselves on video-tape and to read the examiners' comments. And Cable TV put the tapes on the air, although I suspect the viewing audience was pretty small.

I repeated the same procedure with forty-four students in four sessions in the winter term, this time going even further afield for external examiners. Associate Dean Marilyn Williamson of Wayne State University drove in from Detroit, Professor Fredrica Bartz, chairman of English on our branch campus, drove down from Flint, and Ms. Deborah Andrews of Ohio State's English Department drove up all the way from Columbus to examine my students. Only Jay Robinson, chairman of the Literary College English Department, and the engineers from local industry were from Ann Arbor, and this time the engineers invited the whole Ann Arbor Engineers Club to attend. There were even a few high school seniors in the audience.

So much for the evolution of this system. What have been the results?

During this last year I had eighty students. In forty-three of the cases the engineers and the non-engineers recommended identical grades: seventeen A-A's, twenty-four B-B's, two C-C's. In thirty-three cases they differed by only one grade. In twenty-six cases the engineers gave higher grades than the non-engineers; fourteen

A-B's, twelve B-C's. In seven cases the non-engineers gave higher grades than the engineers: seven A-B's. In only four cases did the engineers recommend a grade two notches higher than the non-engineers: four A-C's.

That strikes me as pretty good agreement, although you will notice that the non-engineers tended to follow the curve, giving twenty-four A's, thirty-eight B's, and eighteen C's, while the engineers did not, giving thirty-five A's, forty-three B's, and only two C's. One might attribute this to the fact that the non-engineers were all drawn from the teaching profession and thus tended to be more critical. But there is some evidence to confute this. One of the engineers is presently teaching while acting as president of his own company. He awarded seven A's, three B's, and one C. Another taught at the University of Michigan for several years before becoming a consulting engineer. He awarded two A's and nine B's.

When the two external examiners' grades differed, I turned to evaluations handed in by graduate students of the Engineering Honor Society, Tau Beta Pi, who were also invited to evaluate the students, although they had no opportunity to read the report. I used the average grade they recommended to determine which of the two external examiners' grades I should use. In the case of the four A-C's, I simply split the difference and gave the student a B.

The student reaction to this system seems to be generally favorable. I can recall only two students in the thirteen classes graded this way who complained that they should have received an A rather than a B. I always make it a point to explain the system at the very first class meeting and urge those who prefer to be graded in the more traditional manner to transfer to another instructor. Since we now offer a number of sections, to transfer poses no problem, but rarely does a student do so. Many of them seem to welcome the challenge of facing an external examiner.

My own reaction to this system is somewhat unexpected. I find that I am no longer so certain of my own evaluation of the student's ability. Several times in these seven terms I have been surprised by the external examiners rating a student better than I personally would have rated him. Curiously, and fortunately, I have yet to be surprised by ratings *lower* than I would have given. I have tried to analyze why my impressions differed from those of the external examiners and have tentatively concluded that I have been concentrating so hard on the student's deficiencies during the term in an effort to correct them that I have lost sight of his virtues. I have seen the student every week for fourteen weeks, but in rehearsal conditions where he was sometimes late, sometimes unkempt, sometimes unprepared. All these impressions are stored, like it or not, in my memory and enter, like it or not, into my judgment. But the student has been getting ready for the opening curtain, the big game, the final product. And this is all the external examiner sees and hears—the student on his best behaviour under fire.

This is the real point of the whole system; it separates teaching from evaluation. This is especially important in the teaching of an art or a skill. If one is teaching facts or procedures in which the number of possible choices can be constrained and structured, it is fairly easy to devise a test which will demonstrate persuasively how many facts the student has learned or how accurately he can perform the procedures. The final examination I took in histology as a senior in college was a very simple and very accurate one. I was faced with a room full of microscopes, each one focused on a different slide. Identify each of the tissues on those slides. The greater the number I could identify correctly, the better my grade. The Army test I took as an automotive mechanic was equally simple and accurate. Here is a truck which has been deliberately disabled. Start it up and drive it away. I either could or I couldn't.

When the number of possible choices becomes multiple, as it does in the arts, including writing and speaking, the instructor teaches not only facts and procedures but how to make choices. And many of the options available are only slightly different from one another; so sometimes a decision is based on instinct or prejudice. Since the end product of the art is based upon an interlocking fabric of options selected, the student may have selected a series of options which the instructor would not have selected. The question then becomes, whose instinct or prejudice is better, the student's or the teacher's? To ask the teacher himself to make this decision is to ask him to judge himself against the student.

This is why there has lately been a growing interest in "outside" grading, as witness the report by the Group for Human Development in Higher Education cited in the March 18, 1974, *Chronicle for Higher Education*, or for "credentialling" as suggested in Richard Leuba's article in the February 1975 issue of *Engineering Education*. I am personally persuaded that this is the way to go, especially for the profession of English which is now being roundly criticized for its lack of professionalism.

I can think of no group more appropriate to lead the way toward greater professionalism in the teaching of English than those presently teaching technical writing. They are already accustomed to working, sometimes formally, sometimes informally, with persons outside the English Department. They are already accustomed to having their students' papers read by people in another department. Many of them have come from industry, or work part-time for industry, where an external judgment of one's product is the norm, rather than the exception.

It is for this reason that I have described my experience with this external examiner system. I hope it may persuade other teachers of technical writing to follow the same path.

APPENDIX

HUMANITIES 499—SCIENTIFIC AND TECHNICAL COMMUNICATION
FINAL ORAL PRESENTATIONS

Monday evening, 9 December 1974, Room 1042 East Engineering

7:00 PM   Joseph Soleimanv—Senior in Mechanical Engineering
PERFORMANCE EVALUATION OF ELECTRIC CONTROLLER FOR ELEVATORS OF AC-9 AIRCRAFT

7:15 PM   Richard Sinclair—Senior in Electrical & Computer Engineering
ELECTRONIC MUSIC SYNTHESIZER: PROGRESS REPORT ON DESIGN AND CONSTRUCTION

7:30 PM   Philip Johnson—Senior in Chemical Engineering
SEWAGE WASTES: PRACTICAL USES

7:45 PM   Michael Strayer—Senior in Nuclear Engineering
HAZARDS TO FLOATING NUCLEAR POWER PLANTS: ANALYSIS OF WATERBORNE COMMERCE

8:00 PM   Alexander Brankiewicz—Senior in Chemical Engineering
SULFUR RECOVERY PLANT FOR OIL REFINERY: OPTIMIZATION OF DESIGN PARAMETERS TO MEET EPA REQUIREMENTS

8:15 PM   Kenneth Hawley—Senior in Industrial and Operations Engineering
SIMULATION OF HOSPITAL ADMISSIONS BY COMPUTER: THE DESIGN AND USE OF A MODEL SCHEDULING AND CONTROL SYSTEM

8:30 PM   Darrel Field—Senior in Electrical and Computer Engineering
SINGLE SIDEBAND RADIO SIGNAL GENERATION: A 1974 IMPLEMENTATION OF THE THIRD METHOD OF MODULATION

8:45 PM   John Hinch—Senior in Atmospheric and Oceanic Science
LAKE MICHIGAN LOWER BASIN CURRENTS AND SEDIMENTS: A LITERATURE SURVEY OF RELATIONSHIPS

9:00 PM   Michael Tsuchida—Senior in Engineering Science
*RESPIRATORY TRANSPORT: THE EFFECTS OF pH ON
OXYGEN AFFINITY OF THE BLOOD PIGMENTS HEMOGLOBIN
AND HEMORYTHRIN*

9:15 PM   John Geissman—Graduate Student in Geology
*PALEOMAGNETIC SURVEY OF BUTTE ORE DISTRICT, BUTTE,
MONTANA, WITH APPLICATION TO GEOLOGIC STRUCTURE*

9:30 PM   Charles White—Senior in Chemical Engineering
*WASTE WATER AND PROCESS WATER TREATMENT IN
BREWERIES: COMPARISON OF EFFICIENCIES*

9:45 PM   Peter Fenyes—Senior in Mechanical Engineering
*LIQUID FILM THICKNESS MEASUREMENT: DESIGN AND
IMPLEMENTATION OF A CAPACITANCE PROBE*

External
Examiners: Prof. Milton Foster   Jerome R. Koupal
             Chairman   Chief Mechanical Engineer
             English Department   Bechtel Associates Prof. Corp.
             Eastern Michigan University Ann Arbor, Michigan

and student members of Tau Beta Pi, Engineering Honorary Society

PART FIVE

Viewpoints
in
Technical
Communication

CHAPTER 12

The Trouble with Technical Writing Is Freshman English

DR. W. EARL BRITTON
Department of Humanities
College of Engineering
The University of Michigan

There is so much wrong with freshman English and so much right about technical writing that I suggest they trade places in the academic scene. This exchange would reverse the present arrangement by requiring technical writing courses of all college students, who could then elect specialty subjects like essay and creative writing if they wished.

I'll begin with the weaknesses of the English course normally given to freshmen.

1. It concentrates on the composition of essays, often in connection with assigned readings, and usually in the form of responses to the material. Insofar as the assignments focus on thought and logic, they have point; but I begin to have my

doubts when the emphasis turns to originality and something vaguely labeled literary quality. And there is the matter of the essay itself. Is it realistic to build a writing course around a form of composition that is rarely if ever pursued by the graduate in his professional life?

2. The direction of the writing, that is, the flow of information, proceeds from an ill-informed freshman to a well-informed instructor, primarily because the instructor insists that it be that way. He argues that he can assist the student only by knowing more about the material than the writer does.

3. The emphasis in these essays rests on thought quality and rarely upon communicative effectiveness. It would be absurd to derogate thoughtfulness in writing, but not to challenge a student with the task of explaining a difficult concept or situation to a reader who does not understand or is unacquainted with the matter is to ignore one of the primary requirements of the educated person.

4. Most freshman essays are planned along the inductive pattern. The writer begins at the beginning of his concept and gradually adds to it until finally, at the end, the point of the piece may emerge. The deductive pattern rarely occurs to him, and if it did, would probably be struck down by his instructor. Only recently I heard a colleague condemn a student for blurting out his main idea in the opening sentences.

So much for the obvious limitations of freshman English. Before turning to the virtues of tech writing, I must define my terms.

As all know, we labor in our field under the burden of a misleading name. The term "technical writing" is a far from accurate description of what we do, and turns away many would-be friends because of misunderstanding. Teachers of tech writing courses have regularly occupied a secondary place in the faculty hierarchy. In many instances, only the unfortunate or defenseless members of the staff have been assigned these courses. And the same has been true in Great Britain and on the Continent. Fortunately, this condition is fading; our courses and texts have been improving, we have attracted into the field some very able teachers, and the whole quality of our work has been on the upgrade. But we continue to be misunderstood.

The main reason for this unfortunate condition is the defining of types of writing by their subject matter, as evident in the organizations devoted to medical writing, business writing, science writing, and, more generally, technical writing. The ultimate in misinterpretation is the assumption that a teacher of tech writing teaches technical terminology. If defining tech writing by subject matter does not work, then what does?

I am convinced that the only precise definition of our field lies in specifying our approach. I can think of nothing that can be described as exclusively a technical subject. I think the only accurate view is that we approach our subject technically, and the subject can be anything—all the way from abstruse poetry to the mechanisms of hardware.

About Technical Writing

If this be true, then what is unique about technical writing? I prefer to think its uniqueness lies in the effort of the writer to achieve absolute precision, however impossible this may be. It differs from literature in that more than one interpretation is unacceptable. Literature, music, and the other arts evoke more than one response, sometimes contrary responses, and there is no objection to such richness. But technical writing must be as exact as the directions for firing a missile. A symphony may have different meanings, but a bugle call would be disastrous if it had more than one.

This definition has the merit of avoiding the confusion resulting from defining tech writing by its subject matter. The substance continues to be important, but serves only to specify the area in which the writing occurs. By this approach it becomes meaningful to refer to tech writing in medicine, tech writing in business, and tech writing in engineering. All have in common their precision; they are unique only in their material.

With this clarification in mind, let me return to the support of my thesis by naming the good things about tech writing.

1. Tech writing places the emphasis where it should be: on the reader rather than the writer. Freshman English instructors tend to grade a student's theme on the basis of what it reveals about the student's thinking; tech writing is graded on the basis of what the reader derives from it. The emphasis lies always on the clarity and validity of the communication.

2. The information flows in the correct direction: from knowledge to ignorance. The only reason for such writing is to acquaint

someone with what he does not know or needs to know. The writer writes because he is the one who knows.

3. Tech writing is intellectually taxing. I am puzzled by the critics of tech writing courses who feel that the writing assignments are demeaning. On the contrary, they are extremely demanding. They require far more effort and care than does a casual discussion of one's personal reactions to a published piece regarding our permissive culture, which is the sort of thing often found in freshman essays.

The eminent Shakespearean scholar, G. B. Harrison, has testified to the fact that it is far more difficult to write satisfactory orders for a military operation than to discuss the psychoses of Hamlet, and he has done both. Precision is always achieved with great difficulty and requires the utmost discipline of thought and expression. If you have ever tried to write a set of procedures involving multiple simultaneous operations, you know what I mean. How labored are the statements of lawyers in their understandable effort to be explicit and precise. Nearer home, surely you have witnessed committees unable to agree on the precise meaning of the wording of their report. Usually they wind up, especially in English departments, by stripping away all precision so that the statement is meaningless enough to be acceptable to all parties.

4. And that brings us to another significant feature of tech writing. Its success and effectiveness are measurable, which is more than can be said about the average essay. The reactions to and within an essay are normally personal and subjective; the understanding of tech writing is mental. Its success as communication is quickly evident.

5. Finally, there is far greater likelihood that one can transfer to essay writing the lessons he learns in tech writing than the reverse. Good technical writing requires the exploitation of all the rhetorical devices of focus, logical partitioning and classification, and illuminating sequence, to name a few of the features appropriate to all writing.

In view, then, of these virtues of tech writing in contrast to the objectionable features of freshman English, you will understand why I contend that the trouble with tech writing is freshman English. When I try to teach tech writing to students who have had the conventional first year course, I run smack into all the characteristics that I have labeled as wrong about the course.

The worst feature is the student's insistence upon writing *up to his point* instead of *down from it*. I mean, he proceeds inductively rather than deductively. And this fault extends right on into the Ph.D. dissertation, in which the writer drags us through all the *how he did it's* and perhaps at the end will tell us what it's all about. The research for a dissertation is conducted inductively, but the arrangement should be reversed in the presentation of the material. We should be told the problem, the solution or answer, and then the supporting evidence. In this sequence, the reader can understand and evaluate the various steps in the investigation as he proceeds through the document. But he must know in advance what all the fuss is leading to. The worst fault I find in Ph.D. dissertations is the writer's insistence upon writing it the way he did it. Most dissertations could profit by taking a lesson from the technical report—for the dissertation, after all, is just that, whatever its subject matter.

In suggesting that tech writing replace freshman English as the required writing course, I must offer one modification. The course should be scheduled for the senior year after the student has accumulated a body of knowledge with which to deal. In our department we moved the course to the senior year a while back and are pleased with the results. It's a delight to read papers prepared by well-informed authors.

In conclusion, let me point to a possible irony ahead. Some years ago, decades now, colleges and universities pretty much abandoned rhetoric, especially in its applied form, in favor of linguistic studies. But those who needed rhetoric refused to accept this state of affairs. Professional schools like engineering and business and societies like STC and Medical Writers clung to the study and practice of rhetoric as a tool of communication, and in their hands it has flourished. Wouldn't it be ironical if the universities should now realize that this discipline was not such a bad thing after all and begin reinstituting it in their curricula, as some already are doing, only to discover that the discipline had endured and remained vigorous under the careful protection and nurture of our sometimes despised technical writing groups.

CHAPTER 13

Readability Techniques for Authors and Editors

FRANCES J. LANER
Senior Technical Editor
Technical Information Office
Rockwell International, Rocky Flats Plant *

Pointing out the advantages of readability research studies in a publications program, the writer stresses the importance of such
knowledge to achieve optimum results. From a personal review of
journalism courses, and a survey of editors in various communication programs, the writer notes a considerable lack of knowledge of
readability research among communicators. The principal concern
of all communicators should relate to the improvement of
exchanges between individuals or groups. Many methods and
techniques have been devised for such exchanges, yet limited use
has been made of the basic principles in readability studies which
serve to produce reader impact. Exchanges or sharing of ideas relate

* Work performed under the U.S. Energy Research and Development
Administration Contract E(29-2)3533.

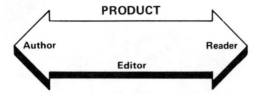

Figure 1. The communication spectrum.

to a communication process. The word *communication* comes from the Latin *communis* meaning common. In any common exchange between individuals, a remarkable phenomenon occurs—the individuals grow. Mature communicators heed the growth patterns along the way, and learn to create for themselves and others the rich experiences of mind and heart. Clutching the ideas gained in an exchange, contemplating their value, and transforming them into a material form result in lasting actualities of *words* on paper.

Thus, a simple act of exchange through the communication process (writing) becomes valuable for its own sake. The author (sender) becomes the principal sharer who transforms or shapes growth in a reader (receiver). Many senders, especially the immature, overlook the basic role of the sender within this frame-work. To identify the act of exchange or sharing, use will be made of the following example referred to as THE COMMUNICATION SPECTRUM (Figure 1).

In Figure 1, a third constant has been interjected, *the Editor*. The discussion will show how the relationship of author-to-editor can produce an environment of growth for the reader if both are cognizant of how to serve the reader. Perhaps a form of visualization from an everyday setting would help to stress the roles of each individual author-editor-reader (Figure 2).

Being aware of the problems of the reader and knowing something of the reader's habits, the editor can translate these to the author. Thus the editor (bartender) in his role serves as the bridge between author and reader to bring them together. In general, authors of technical products are not expected to have an equivalent background in journalism fields which are part of the editor's training, whereas a technical editor may be required to also have a background in some of the areas of concern to the author, and especially in specific scientific disciplines. Through knowledge of readability research, the editor can provide the author with techniques which will enhance and improve the communication product being prepared. The key to this endeavor relates primarily to *reader habits*, and capitalizing on such knowledge.

Figure 2. "My author does not understand me."

Readability Studies

Readability refers to research in human communication. The topic is far too broad for coverage in a single presentation, but the items selected have been emphasized to whet the interest of communicators in pursuing additional background. Readability research studies should not be confused with the term *readability surveys*, which in general are brief surveys of reader reactions. In most cases, such surveys are inadequately prepared and analyzed to give accurate data. The materials selected have been taken from two important publications which are recommended to all communicators for complete study [1, 2].

In the book by George R. Klare, some 480 studies are reported [1]. The projects are explained, analyzed, and evaluated for use in specific studies. The author introduces three areas in which the term "readability" has been used.

1. Legibility of handwriting or typography.
2. Reading ease related to interest value or the pleasantness of writing.
3. Ease of understanding or comprehension based on the style of writing.

For purposes of technical programs, the third area has more importance and will be stressed. Nevertheless, a brief discussion will also be made on how under Item 1, the third area can be served [2].

Research studies under Item 3 describe a variety of methods as formulas designed to measure comprehension, theory, construction, and validation of formulas, applications of principles, formulas to writing, etc. Formulas are merely practical devices which give a quantitative estimate of readability, and users should be alerted that their use was never intended to make good writers. Primarily, a formula is a means of rating a piece of writing after it has been written. Writing is an art, not a science. Certain principles can be taught and followed to develop good writing, and one principle overlooked by many writers refers to the collection of adequate knowledge about the reader. Readable writing, of course, does relate to content and style. However, the merit of various styles usually takes on a more personal objective rather than impersonal interpretations based on research, so will not be emphasized. Since the reader is a human being (usually), he has certain habits similar to mine or yours. Thus as a communicator serving the reader, one can judge some of his actions. For example, something will be known about the educational level, the technical or nontechnical background of the reader, or the particular interest or motivation of the reader for certain materials. In a sense, authors set goals based on reader understanding, learning, or efficiency, or should do so. Unfortunately, many do not set such goals, and write for the sake of writing. With a better knowledge of the reader, goals can be set and materials can be prepared to increase reader interest, speed, comprehension, and efficiency.

The habits of readers have been well documented through the ages. One of the first groups concerned with the reader was the Talmudists (900 AD), religious education leaders who would examine early texts to be certain that the word and idea count were contributing to better understanding and not to the fog index. In 1840, vocabularies were studied in relation to children's books, *The McGuffey Readers*. In 1893, L. A. Sherman made a study of sentence length quantitatively as an indicator of style [3]. He analyzed average sentence lengths used by famous writers. He found that sentence lengths had been decreasing from fifty words during the early period (down to Elizabethan times) to about twenty-three; and also found a decrease in predication or conversely, an increase in simple sentences. Sentence length did not become an object of study as the development of formulas began, but did become introduced again later. Today, the study of sentence length can even be used to settle disputes in authorship.

In 1921, E. L. Thorndike developed a *Teacher's Word Book* which still has use today [4]. Word lists are used extensively by textbook publishers, encyclopedia companies, and many educational groups. From Thorndike's work, the stage was set for studies which led to the development of formulas. With these bases, Lively and Pressey in 1923 developed the first method of measuring readability, considered as a formula [5]. Thus vocabulary was agreed upon by researchers as an important factor in reading difficulty. Although the first studies concerned mostly books of children, the librarians in the middle 20's gave impetus to work efforts to find readable material for adults. Then later extensions of this work were made to educational needs for grade placement, etc. The topics are too comprehensive to discuss fully, but more detail can be found in Klare's listings of the major contributions by some twenty or more authors [1]. Specifically, the works of R. F. Flesch and R. Gunning will be of interest [6-8].

Reader Success

Readability poses a direct communication problem since the need for readability increases with size and variability of the intended audience. Levels of readability become of major importance also and the principle of least effort operates almost with a vengeance on the writer. Thus to ensure reader success, an assessment of many elements must be made in predicting the difficulty or the facility of reviewing a communication product. Such elements include *content, style, format,* and *organization*. The first two have been alluded to earlier and have more importance than the others. However, in any assessment of a work, all of the elements must be given attention. To diagnose the element of style, an understanding of the units (language) of analysis is a prerequisite.

Units of Analysis

The basic unit, both as a formula factor and as a measure of length, is the *word*. A smaller unit also known as the type space has been designated as the *letter*. A whole thesis could be written on these two units alone, but, to move to another formula factor, consider the *syllable*. Syllables have been shown to correspond to breath impulses while reading, and certain conclusions can be drawn from such studies assessing the ease or tension of the reader. Next the count of groups of words enters the equation, and lastly the full sentence. No units beyond the sentence in size have been used in readability studies. Because of space limitations, results from content and style research on the units can not be detailed.

Some astounding facts about reader habits are provided in the literature and should be reviewed by all communicators.

In addition to the knowledge on the units, the techniques or methods used to display them have significance. The topic involves readability research in the area under Item 1, the *Legibility of Typography*. Typography focuses on the elements of format and organization which are easier to demonstrate in an article than the elements of content and style. Display of words or letters can increase or decrease readability through various methods which include frequency or recognition factors, use of visuals, page arrangements, etc. The book by Tinker offers some 240 studies in this area [2]. To simplify the discussion, a specific example will be taken of a communication product produced in my day-to-day work assignments, the *Technical Research Report*. A measure of success has been attained in this respect, and the techniques are recommended for all types of publications as the reader does not change his habits from one kind of communication to another.

The Technical Research Report

The report example serves as a communication product which publishes the results of technical and scientific research funded by the Energy Research and Development Administration at the Rocky Flats Plant in Golden, Colorado [9]. The Plant operates under contract to the Atomics International Division of Rockwell International. Distribution of the report includes a broad audience of both internal and external scientific and managerial readers. Such reports take many forms, but each original draft from technical authors is reviewed by an editor for content and style before being sent to the production groups. At each stage of preparation, a knowledgeable editor in readability research can prescribe procedures based on known reader habits. Authors may not become involved initially, but during review of galleys, the editor has an opportunity to introduce and point out benefits in page arrangements of all elements based on readability studies.

Before proceeding to galley or page-proof stages, the initial evaluation of a product must be made. The first concern is directed to the class or category of a printed work, i.e., whether it is a formal or informal product. As a communication product, the *technical report* has been classed as a formal product, as opposed to informal ones such as bulletins, newsletters, newspapers, magazines, etc. Whatever the class, concern must be directed to parts of the product and the order of priorities for each part as noted:

PARTS:

1. Text	4. Title	7. Captions
2. Date	5. References	8. Page Numbers
3. Author	6. Art Work	

The first three items should never be subordinated to the remaining parts of any publication. Text or content must always be prime. In a sense, the items from 4 through 8 could be omitted entirely. When text has good continuity and description, not much else is needed. Except for convention, page numbers could be deleted completely. They have the least priority of all parts, yet many publications go overboard in displaying page numbers. The treatment only serves to distract and slow down the reader. When a publication, however, has been prepared to function only as a special issue, many of the priorities can be juggled. No one should ever become a slave to the methods or techniques, but make use of them based on the function of a publication.

Once the function of a publication is known, then the elements of content and style are examined. When satisfactory, the technical report moves through the production processes where considerations of format and organization receive special emphasis based on reader habits to enhance impact of the product, and keep the reader pleased and relaxed during a reading session.

Reader Habits

Research studies have been conducted with various devices and methods and, in some cases, electronic scanners are used to record the movement of the eyes when a subject begins a reading session. At the same time, a record of breathing impulses of the reader reveals either tension or ease as responses. Without exception, all western readers viewing a page or a cover will focus the eyes on the left-hand corner of the piece and proceed on down the page along a diagonal direction to the right. To capitalize on this habit, segments are placed along the diagonal to capture attention. Publishers and advertisers aware of this principle often make use of it in planning materials.

Displaying type faces in various positions on the page (vertical versus horizontal), and also in selections of the size, shape, and density of type faces produce an effect on readers. In addition, the placement of all such elements on a page produces effects. To illustrate, examine Figure 3 in which the dark areas in the square and the circle represent text or content. Findings show that when

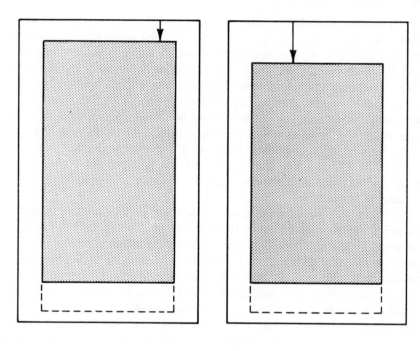

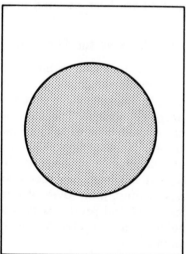

Figure 3.

the eyes focus on a circle, they never stay within the circle, but dart back and forth all over the page, and outside of the page. These movements increase eye fatigue, whereas when the eyes view a page with material in a square, they seldom go outside the corners

of the square, nor off the page, but always within the boundaries.
Thus less eye fatigue occurs. During these scanning operations, the
breathing of the readers has been recorded and has given clues as
to fatigue or ease. Thus, text type, if carefully chosen, can help the
reader, because shapes of text type produce effects on the eye,
as the circle or the square. For example, when a publication uses
sans serif type faces (clean line letters without strokes as h, w), the
eyes react the same as when viewing a circle. They do not stay
with the text type, whereas, when *serif* type faces (letters with
strokes, h, w) are used, the eye movement is captured, remains
with the text and absorbs meanings, and there is less tension and
fatigue of the reader.

Another way to increase reader attention concerns margin uses.
Viewing Figure 3 again, note the spacing at the top of the pages
(arrows) in the squares. Research shows that when a reader can
begin at the top of a page with minimum space, he will proceed
quickly into the text. With more space at the top, he hesitates
before reading on, and even looks away from the page. A wider
margin at the bottom of a page appears to rest him and his
breathing is with less tension, and he turns the page without delay.
If the margin is small, he delays. Many other considerations on page
arrangement and margin have been covered in the research studies.

Art Work versus Text Flow

Assigning the priority to text in a publication provides another
means to capitalize on reader responses. In Figure 4, several two-
page spread arrangements illustrate how text flow receives prime
treatment over art work (A and B). The dark areas in the left
illustration represent an even flow of text to help the reader keep
attention on the content. He does not need to jump over an
illustration or reroute his eyes to pick up the text. In the right and
bottom illustrations, text has been obstructed by the insertion of
art work, and the reader must jump over objects to continue
reading. This reduces speed and produces fatigue. The placement of
captions with art includes another area in which reader speed and
interest can be enhanced.

Figure 5 illustrates a page arrangement in which captions above
the center line of a page are inserted under the art. Below the
center line, captions are inserted above the visuals. The result gives
clean lines at top and bottom which serve to please the reader.
Readers are not conscious of these reactions, but research clearly
shows definite responses which increase or reduce reader efficiency.

The communicator, at this point, might throw up his hands and

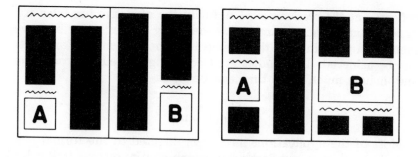

Figure 4. Flow of text versus illustrations.

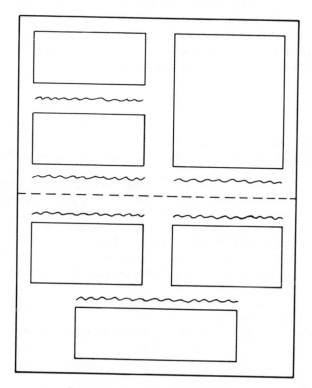

Figure 5. Treatment of captions.

reflect: *Let the reader swim!* Actually the objective has been to expose you to the research areas providing resources for improvement, and to point out the savings in manpower and effort that can be achieved. The studies are fascinating as well as productive and include much more than can be given.

Conclusions

Most of the applications have been directed to the formal technical report, a publication in which continuous reading is both voluntary and required in work assignments by technicians and scientists in a company. Thus, the concern for the reader would be greater than for publications read merely for recreation. In general, neither authors nor editors study in depth what the needs of the reader are or how best to serve him. To communicate work results, authors and editors must spend some time learning about the readers just as a brain surgeon must learn about his patients and how best to serve them after he has learned the skills of his practice. No short cut exists except to learn the art of writing from planning, constructing, joining, polishing, conquering the problems arising from sentences, sounds, ideas, arrangements, divisions, and all the rest. Author and editor excelling in the art of writing must not omit prime considerations of capturing the reader. If the reader's habits and needs are not analyzed, both author and editor become as the surgeon with no patients.

REFERENCES

1. G. R. Klare, *The Measurement of Readability*, Third Printing, Iowa State University Press, Ames, Iowa, 1969.
2. M. A. Tinker, *Legibility of Print*, Second Printing, Iowa State University Press, Ames, Iowa, 1964.
3. L. A. Sherman, The Literary Sentence Length in English Prose, Chapter XIX, The Decrease of Predication, Chapter XX, *Analytics of Literature*, Ginn and Company, Boston, Massachusetts, pp. 256-268, 1893.
4. E. L. Thorndike, *A Teacher's Word Book*, 1921; and *A Teacher's Word Book of 30,000 Words*, 1944, Teachers College, Columbia University, New York.
5. B. A. Lively and S. L. Pressey, A Method for Measuring the "Vocabulary Burden" of Textbooks, *Educational Administration and Supervision*, 9, p. 389, October 1923.
6. R. F. Flesch, A New Readability Yardstick, *Journal of Applied Psychology*, 32, p. 221, June 1948.
7. R. F. Flesch, Measuring the Level of Abstraction, *Journal of Applied Psychology*, 34, p. 384, December 1958.

8. R. Gunning, *The Technique of Clear Writing*, McGraw-Hill Book Company, New York, 1952.
9. F. J. Laner, Producing Quality Technical Research Reports, Panel 4B, The State of Technical Writing, Society for Technical Communications, *Proceedings of the 18th International Technical Communications Conference*, San Francisco, California, June 2-5, 1971.

CHAPTER 14

Motivating Students with a Winning Assignment

DR. L. P. DRISKILL
Department of English
Rice University

Creating interesting and appropriate assignments continues to challenge technical writing instructors. Textbook assignments often lack immediacy; they "don't seem real." Students find it difficult to imagine a specific audience for their writing. Many students lack work experience that could help them anticipate the writing demands of future jobs and find relevance in their writing assignments. Even vivid assignments raggedly fit the varying needs and backgrounds of the mechanical engineers, botanists, computer science majors, metallurgists, and other specialists who enroll in technical writing classes.

Assignments focusing on different writing skills may seem unrelated. Narrating a problem, describing a process, and constructing tables and charts may begin to seem like no more than the particular topics taught some Monday or Wednesday. Technical writing instructors need assignments that integrate skills and, like all teachers, they long for assignments that will turn their students on to language and generate commitment and enthusiasm for the course.

Stimulating Assignment

For the past two years, members of the technical writing class at Rice University have tackled a major assignment that has stimulated student interest and enthusiasm, pulled together in a single assignment many of the skills taught in the course, and earned prestige for the class and its members.

This assignment gives immediate relevance to most of the skills taught throughout the semester. At the end of the fifth week of class, students must turn in a memorandum describing an actual problem or question they wish to investigate as a feasibility study, outlining the schedule they expect to follow in the investigation, and requesting the instructor's approval. Students are aware that a feasibility study must result in a decision or recommendation and must be organized to help the reader accept the writer's recommendation. By this time, the class has become familiar with the basic skills they need to begin their investigation. The class has covered technical correspondence, reviewed basic expository techniques, written process descriptions, discussed methods of conducting interviews, and practiced using basic bibliographical reference tools in the sciences and the branches of engineering.

Over the next four weeks students practice additional skills essential to producing their final feasibility study. They write an investigative report and two five-to-ten page feasibility studies based on situations and data found in the text. The preparatory nature of these assignments is stressed and students are urged to find similarities between the discussions, tables, styles, and other features of these assignments and their own projects. Class discussions focus on the implications of a key concept in the course, reader-oriented writing: alternate patterns of organization for different audiences of readers; variations in information needs; desirable alterations in style; and overall graphics, tables, and charts that facilitate the reader's comprehension and judgment-making. For example, students learn that if a study deals with a three-year solution to a problem, tables showing costs should include three-year figures computed to help the reader understand the overall cost of the program as well as its yearly cost (or whatever intervals are appropriate for the reader). Each student chooses a particular audience for his or her report and begins to appraise that audience's needs, deciding what those individuals will need or wish to know to understand and approve the report's recommendation. Information-gathering begins and after class discussions of progress reports, students submit a four-week progress report on their investigations, measuring their progress against their original schedule.

Topics Chosen

The topics chosen reveal the wide variety of student interests, concerns, talents, and expertise. Probably the freedom to select for approval a personally interesting project or problem contributes most to the students' motivation. Most of the feasibility studies attack problems of concern to the university. The school's vulnerability to the rising costs of utilities was of interest to several students who investigated the feasibility of various ameliorative steps including:

1. use of a small nuclear reactor's cooling system to produce steam for generating electricity;
2. use of solar energy, and
3. use of wind-driven power generators.

The last solution was studied by a woman who involved other senior mechanical engineers in designing a generator superior in efficiency to present commercial models. The installation of the generator recommended by the study (now accepted) will lower the costs of room and board at the residential college where the generator will be installed by $200 per student each year, a significant saving for most students.

Other studies weighed the efficacy of proposed ways of increasing the university library's shelving capacity, the establishment of a stop-smoking clinic on campus (funded and ready to start soon), the installation of lights on the tennis courts, the comparative costs of two building designs for additions to the gymnasium, the creation of a laser link between the university and the Texas Medical Center's communications system a few blocks away, energy savings to be recovered from shutting down various loops or portions of the university air-conditioning system in summer, and alternative architectural designs for study areas in a residential college. One study evaluated the feasibility of resolving a particularly odious annual problem, dealing with the droppings of several hundred thousand migrating blackbirds who roost on campus for several weeks each spring, by turning the droppings into a marketable neutralized fertilizer. "From problem to profit"

was a recurrent theme; two civil engineering students investigated
the feasibility of developing land owned by the university for a
residential subdivision.

Some students tackled community problems. One pair of
students investigated the feasibility of obtaining public service time
on television and radio to run spots on infant care and infant
health problems. Another student surveyed the annual seafood
catch of major companies operating in Freeport, a town on the
Gulf of Mexico, to determine the feasibility of building and
operating a freezer plant that would boost the town's economy. A
survey of farmers and other potential users, interviews, and estimates
of building and equipment costs yielded a professional report
addressed to the mayor and city council.

Other students turned to present or recent summer job experiences to deal with an actual industrial problem. Students tested the
feasibility of using a new wharf design, selected a filtering device
for a chemical plant's effluent treatment, evaluated a desalination
process that could be installed in a nuclear generating plant, and
compared ways of stabilizing an industrial building that was
becoming unsafe through cracking caused by the movement of an
active geological fault. A few students pursued questions of personal
concern, investigating the feasibility of different senior independent
research projects, and off-campus versus on-campus living costs.

Investigating this wide range of topics gives students practical
experience, experience in devising indices or measures that provide
a suitable basis for decision-making; experience in the practical
difficulties of information gathering; and experience in presenting
information for particular audiences. Due three weeks before the
end of the semester, the written feasibility studies become the
basis of oral presentations given for the class during the final class
meetings. The early due date means that students give adequate
attention to the preparation of the feasibility study, which is
complete before they must write most other term papers and
prepare for final exams.

Oral Presentations

Oral presentations of reports to the class are videotaped. A
brief group discussion of what the student has done best and what
he or she needs to improve follows each presentation immediately.
Earlier class discussions have emphasized techniques for adapting
reports for oral presentation: simplifying sentence structure,
repeating key terms, using visual aids, and using appropriate body

language. Students bring these concepts to bear in discussing their friends' presentations. The videotapes are put on reserve so that students privately can "see themselves as others see them," and become thoroughly familiar with their own mannerisms.

REWARDING ASPECTS

The oral presentations have several rewarding aspects. Students get the satisfaction of formally displaying the results of their efforts. Their enthusiasm for their own projects tends to make the reports vivid and interesting to their friends. The class members also represent a different audience than the one for whom the reports were originally written; so the students develop a keener appreciation of how different audiences make different demands on writers.

Students who plan to seek jobs in technical writing are encouraged to revise their feasibility studies and place them in their files to show to interviewing employers. The report provides the employer a review of the best independent work the student can do, and because the feasibility study usually requires a variety of writing skills, it most often contains samples of the skills employers want to check.

Most students work very hard on these projects and give the course good word-of-mouth publicity that stems from their own feelings of satisfaction and accomplishment. From an instructor's point of view, the best result of this program is seeing students discover that if they gather and present information well they can intervene in the system around them. Some students who enroll with the attitude that writing will be the worst part of their engineering or science career emerge confident that writing will be the part of their job that will ensure their future success. The course has acquired a good reputation; more departments are recommending that their students register for the course. The students also have gained prestige on campus. Whereas writing courses in some schools are considered little more than first-aid stations for verbally inept students, the "talking wounded," the members of the technical writing class have come to be seen as an elite. Faculty members, heads of campus offices, and even deans have started sending memoranda asking that next year's students tackle specific problems that need a fresh and thorough evaluation. We have affirmed for a long time that the pen was mightier than the sword; now technical writing students are discovering it is at least equal to the computer, the calculator, and the slide rule.

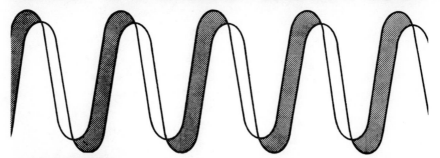